"*Addiction and Virtue* is one of only a few the false dilemma limiting addiction to e more, Dunnington does this from a Chris

Linda Mercadante, author, *Victims & Sinners,* and professor, Theological School in Ohio

"Kent J. Dunnington offers a compelling account of addiction as interpreted through the lens of virtue. A strong theological and philosophical foundation helps the reader to see how the good news of Jesus Christ offers a powerful alternative to the habit of addiction. While some within the addiction treatment community will find Dunnington's arguments controversial, others will experience them as a breath of fresh air. Either way, *Addiction and Virtue* is a worthwhile read!"

Virginia T. Holeman, professor of counseling, Asbury Theological Seminary

"Considerations of addiction as disease are helpful but inadequate. Kent Dunnington shows us that addiction is a habit, more akin to idolatry or wrongful worship. In doing so he deepens our notions of addiction but also enriches our understandings of sin and redemption. I can't think of a more timely subject, or a more exemplary way to do theological ethics."

Sam Wells, dean of the chapel, Duke University

"In *Addiction and Virtue* Kent Dunnington uses Aristotle, Thomas and the philosophically clarified concept of habit to illuminate addiction. The addicts in our midst emerge as 'contemporary prophets' who, if we can but find the ears to hear them, call society as a whole to profound change and the Christian church in particular to renewal. This valuable book points the way, if we are ever to recover from all our junkie-like 'habits' of personal behavior and social interaction, to turn them into truly sustaining habitats for flourishing human life."

Francis F. Seeburger, professor of philosophy, University of Denver

"Drawing on Aristotle's and Aquinas's accounts of habit, Kent Dunnington has given us an analysis of addiction we have desperately needed. Few are able to combine philosophical analysis with theological insight, but Dunnington has done it in a manner that helps us better understand the nature of addiction and why it is so prevalent in our time. This is a book that needs to be read not only by those who work in the fields of addictive behaviors but also by philosophers, theologians and pastors. I suspect in a short amount of time, this book will be viewed as something of a classic in the field."

Stanley Hauerwas, Duke Divinity School

"An intelligent, informed and well-integrated treatment of virtue and addiction that doesn't fall into theological, philosophical or scientific dogma. Dunnington provides a framework that is invaluable for clinicians and researchers in the area of addiction, and for those who strive to live the virtuous life."

William M. Struthers, Ph.D., associate professor of psychology, Wheaton College, and author of *Wired for Intimacy*

STRATEGIC INITIATIVES IN EVANGELICAL THEOLOGY

ADDICTION AND VIRTUE

BEYOND THE MODELS OF DISEASE AND CHOICE

KENT DUNNINGTON

♦

IVP Academic

An imprint of InterVarsity Press
Downers Grove, Illinois

InterVarsity Press
P.O. Box 1400, Downers Grove, IL 60515-1426
World Wide Web: www.ivpress.com
E-mail: email@ivpress.com

InterVarsity Press® is the book-publishing division of InterVarsity Christian Fellowship/USA®, a movement of students and faculty active on campus at hundreds of universities, colleges and schools of nursing in the United States of America, and a member movement of the International Fellowship of Evangelical Students. For information about local and regional activities, write Public Relations Dept., InterVarsity Christian Fellowship/USA, 6400 Schroeder Rd., P.O. Box 7895, Madison, WI 53707-7895, or visit the IVCF website at <www.intervarsity.org>.

Scripture quotations, unless otherwise noted, are from the New Revised Standard Version of the Bible, *copyright 1989 by the Division of Christian Education of the National Council of the Churches of Christ in the USA. Used by permission. All rights reserved.*

While all stories in this book are true, some names and identifying information in this book have been changed to protect the privacy of the individuals involved.

Design: Cindy Kiple

Images: The Magdalen of Sorrow by Paul Cezanne at Musee d'Orsay, Paris, France. Scala/Art Resource, NY.

ISBN 978-0-8308-3901-8

Printed in the United States of America ∞

Library of Congress Cataloging-in-Publication Data

Dunnington, Kent, 1977-
Addiction and virtue: beyond the models of disease and choice /
Kent Dunnington.
p. cm.
Includes bibliographical references and indexes.
ISBN 978-0-8308-3901-8 (pbk.: alk. paper)
1. Habit breaking—Religious aspects—Christianity. 2. Compulsive behavior—Religious aspects—Christianity. 3. Church work with recovering addicts. I. Title.
BV4598.7.D86 2011
259'.429—dc22

2011013643

P   20   19   18   17   16   15   14   13   12   11   10   9   8   7   6   5   4   3   2   1

Y   28   27   26   25   24   23   22   21   20   19   18   17   16   15   14   13   12   11

To

John J. McDermott,

friend and teacher

CONTENTS

◆

PREFACE

◆

Recent years have witnessed a massive growth of research on addiction. In 1962, when the Yale Center of Alcohol Studies was moved to Rutgers University, it was the only research institution of its kind. Today approximately one hundred addiction research centers are housed at major universities across the United States. Most of the work is being done by natural and social scientists. Theologians have written comparatively little on addiction, philosophers even less.

This book inserts philosophy and theology into the investigations taking place within the field of "addiction studies." I argue that efforts to understand and ameliorate addictive behavior have been unnecessarily limited by scientific accounts of addiction. In particular, because so much of the public discourse on addiction is conducted in scientifically reductive terms, many Christians who rightly sense the spiritual significance of addiction are unable to articulate this significance in theologically substantive ways. This book is an attempt to provide such an articulation.

The book defends three broad theses. First, it demonstrates that philosophical analysis of human action is required to clear up many of the conceptual confusions that plague the discourse of addiction studies. Within that discourse, addiction is construed as either a disease or a type of willful choice. Neither of those categories is adequate to the phenomenon of addiction. For instance, the disease concept obscures the extent to which persons may be expected to take responsibility for their addictions, and the choice concept obscures the distinctiveness of the addictive experience. This book argues that the category of "habit" is indispensable for charting an intelligible path between the muddled polarities of "disease" and "choice." The category of habit permits us to describe addiction in a noncontradictory way, without doing violence to the testimonies of persons with addictions.

Human persons develop habits in order to facilitate the pursuit of specific human goods. Thus, if addiction is appropriately characterized as a type of human habit, we may ask about the specific kinds of goods that draw persons into habits of addiction. This is a strange way of speaking; we are so gripped by the destructive effects of addiction that we are not accustomed to considering its constructive appeal. The second broad thesis of the book is that the prevalence and power of addiction indicates the extent to which a society fails to provide nonaddictive modes of acquiring certain kinds of goods necessary to human welfare. Addiction is therefore an embodied critique of the culture which sustains it. I propose that addiction as we understand it is a peculiarly modern habit, and that addiction can be viewed as a mirror reflecting back to us aspects of modern culture that we tend to overlook or suppress. Persons with severe addictions are among those contemporary prophets that we ignore to our own demise, for they show us who we truly are.

Christians must heed prophets. Christians, therefore, are called to appropriately describe the addictive experience and to consider how the church may be complicit in the production of a culture of addiction. To this end, the book endeavors to place addiction within a theological framework. The third broad thesis that the book defends is that the theological category of sin can deepen and extend our understanding of addiction. Addiction is not identical to sin, but neither can it be separated from sin. The power of addiction cannot be adequately appraised until addiction is understood as a misguided enactment of our quest for right relationship with God. I argue that addiction is in fact a sort of counterfeit worship. Thus, although it is true that the church has much to learn from recovery programs such as Alcoholics Anonymous, it is also true that the church has much to offer to the recovery movement and indeed to all of us who struggle with addiction.

I anticipate two possible stumbling blocks for the reader. First, the reader who is expecting a self-help book on addiction may become frustrated by the abstract and theoretical nature of the argument. I will not be providing a psychological portrait of the addictive personality or a list of recovery principles. Nor will I attempt to provide a straightforward causal account of why people engage in addictive behavior. People engage in addictive behavior for all sorts of reasons, including rejection, the loss of a child, family neglect, sexual trauma and victimization, divorce, unemployment, depression, and identity crises involving race, gender or sexuality.[1] Rather than offering an account of why people *engage* in addictive behavior, I am attempting to offer an account of why they *become addicted* to those behaviors. I am attempting to explain why addiction takes on a life of its own, has its own rationality and rhythm, and persists regardless of change in

---

[1]I want to address a concern here that my treatment of addiction without an attending examination of trauma and victimization may lead some readers to feel that their more urgent struggles with addiction are not sufficiently addressed. Others may think that my treatment of addiction is not adequately attentive to issues of gender, race and ethnicity. Each of these issues is indeed relevant to the theme of addiction. Much of what I have to say, particularly in later chapters, will address some of these issues obliquely. However, I have opted not to focus directly on these important intersections, first, because I am not qualified to do so and, second, because dwelling on these matters raises a different set of questions than those which I am pursuing here. To treat these themes with the attention they deserve would require another book (or several). For helpful discussions of the relationship between trauma, victimization and addiction, see Mary Louise Bringle, *Despair: Sickness or Sin?* (Nashville: Abingdon, 1990); and Christine Gudorf, *Victimization: Examining Christian Complicity* (Philadelphia: Trinity Press International, 1992). On the relationship between gender and addiction, see Charlotte Davis Kasl, *Women, Sex, and Addiction* (New York: Harper Paperbacks, 1990).

more immediate circumstances. I am trying to articulate, not the power of alcohol or crack or heroin or pornography, but the power of addiction. My working hypothesis is that there is something philosophically and theologically profound about addiction but that standard and entrenched paradigms must be recast or overthrown in order to bring what is at stake into stark relief.

Second, the reader may be put off by the extent to which the argument leans on Aristotle and Thomas Aquinas. The book grounds itself in a rigorous philosophical analysis of human action that draws primarily from the thought of these two classical thinkers. This is not to satisfy an antiquarian curiosity or to offer a backhanded apologetic for either thinker; I am neither an "Aristotelian" nor a "Thomist," per se. As I began to think about addiction, I found myself returning to these thinkers again and again for a simple reason: both Aristotle and Aquinas assume that the primary task of any philosophy of human action is to explain how it is possible that human beings know the good and yet fail to do it. This is, of course, what is utterly puzzling about addiction—that we should repeatedly and compulsively do that which we know is damaging us. It is because Aristotle and Aquinas remain to this day the most sophisticated and careful students of this puzzle that I have found their work to be so helpful in trying to understand addiction.

The argument proceeds as follows. The first chapter sets the stage by responding to the suspicion and prejudice that is likely to confront any attempt to speak of addiction "philosophically." The prevailing view of the general public, the media, and the majority of those working within the addiction-recovery movement is that addiction is a disease and that, therefore, addiction is a topic for investigation by scientists and physicians but not by philosophers or theologians. I contend that attempts to describe addiction exclusively in the language of science—as "disease"—are bound to fail since they rest on a basic conceptual confusion about what is constitutive of voluntary action.

Chapters two and three develop the view that addiction is neither a disease nor a choice but rather a habit. I am interested in asking what the experience of being addicted can teach us about the complexity of human action, and conversely, how a careful analysis of certain aspects of human agency can illuminate some of the more perplexing elements of addictive experience. The reader should be forewarned that these are the most technical chapters of the book.

Chapter four argues that, contrary to popular belief, addiction is not concerned primarily with sensible goods (hedonic pleasures) but rather with moral and intellectual goods, and chapter five explores the idea that the habit of addiction may be a response to a peculiarly modern lack of certain kinds of moral and intellectual goods. The strategy changes here, from the systematic unfolding of a philosophy of human action in chapters two and three to a more far-ranging and (inevitably) speculative exercise in philosophy of culture.

Chapter six moves into theological territory and addresses the question of whether or not we learn anything of descriptive or normative import by thinking about addiction in terms of the category of sin. Conversely, the chapter considers how our understanding of sin, including the doctrine of original sin, is enriched by our understanding of addiction. Chapter seven is concerned with the relationship between addictive behavior and worship. It contends that addiction offers a powerful response to the modern loss of transcendence. Finally, in chapter eight, I explore the relationship between the church and addiction by proposing what sort of church would be necessary to offer an alternative way of life more compelling than the addicted life.

This book has been a long time in the making. The analysis of addiction from the perspective of the philosophy of action arose out of my dissertation, written under the direction of John J. McDermott. Although he will disagree with the theological dimension of my treatment, I hope that John will see in the book something of the seriousness and sympathy with which he taught me to regard addiction and addicted persons. The book is dedicated to John as a token of my gratitude.

The rest of my committee consisted of Scott Austin, David Erlandson, Reinhard Hütter and Stanley Hauerwas, each of whom was generous with their time and attention. I am especially grateful to David for praying for me throughout the process and in the ensuing years and to Stanley for encouraging me to write this book.

In addition, several people have read all or part of the manuscript along the way. My thanks to John Kiess, Sheila McCarthy, Caleb McDaniel, Clifton Stringer, Johannah Swank, Michael Trapp and Ben Wayman. Special thanks to my mother, Paula Church, the most loyal and caring editor a son could wish for. Each of these friends offered valuable suggestions on the manuscript and heartened me by making the writing process less lonely. Thanks also to an anonymous reader for InterVarsity Press and to editor Gary Deddo for his help in shepherding this project along to completion.

1

ADDICTION AND DISEASE

Science, Philosophy and Theology

◆

What business has a student of philosophy and theology writing a book about addiction? Shouldn't that be left to the experts—the scientists? After all, the prevailing view among researchers, treatment counselors, the media and the general public, is that addiction is a disease.[1] If addictions are diseases, then they are not the sorts of things that humans *do* but rather the sorts of thing that humans *suffer*. And, if this is so, then it would simply be misguided to ask—as I propose to ask—how we should understand and describe addiction as a type of human *action*. It would be misguided because it would be an example of what philosophers call a "category mistake," akin to asking whether the number seven is yellow or green. If it would be mistaken to ask, "What are people doing when they are acting cancerously?" is it not equally mistaken to ask, "What are people doing when they are acting addictively?"

---

[1]The literature on the disease concept of alcoholism is vast. Its seminal text is E. M. Jellinek's *The Disease Concept of Alcoholism* (New Haven, Conn.: Hillhouse Press, 1960). The most impassioned and qualified of its contemporary defenders was Mark Keller, late editor of the *Quarterly Journal of Studies on Alcohol*. See his "The Disease Concept of Alcoholism Revisited," *Journal of Studies on Alcohol* 37 (1976): 1694-1717. The trend-setting Center of Alcohol Studies at Rutgers University and the National Institute on Alcoholism and Alcohol Abuse are both deeply invested in this paradigm, and most of the articles one finds in the several journals of alcoholism and addiction studies either argue for or assume the disease concept of alcoholism.

That philosophers are made anxious by these questions may explain why so few of them have written on addiction. To date, only two philosophical monographs on addiction have been published.[2] Theologians have been similarly reticent, and what has been written in a theological vein is often hampered by conceptual confusions stemming from the hegemony of the disease concept of addiction.[3]

What we need is some conceptual ground-clearing. In order to make room for a philosophical and theological study of addiction, I will demonstrate that every attempt to provide "scientifically objective" necessary and sufficient conditions for addiction has failed. More importantly, I will argue that attempts to define addiction in exclusively medical-scientific terminology—as "disease"—not only *have* failed but in fact are *bound* to fail. The argument proceeds by examining three areas in which science has exerted enormous influence over the discourse on addiction: first, the attempt to define addiction; second, the attempt to assess risk for addiction; and third, the attempt to treat addiction. Although the sciences have made significant contributions in each of these areas, the conclusions that have been drawn from these contributions have been exaggerated in ways that distort our understanding of addiction. I do not deny that science has much of interest and importance to say on the subject of addiction. However, science has not and cannot say everything of interest

---

[2]Francis Seeburger, *Addiction and Responsibility: An Inquiry Into the Addictive Mind* (New York: Crossroad, 1993); and Bruce Wilshire, *Wild Hunger: The Primal Roots of Modern Addiction* (New York: Rowman and Littlefield Publishers, 1998). The late philosopher Herbert Fingarette has written a highly contested book about alcoholism, *Heavy Drinking: The Myth of Alcoholism as a Disease* (Berkeley: University of California Press, 1988), but Fingarette writes mainly as a participant in the field of alcohol studies. A conference titled "What Is Addiction?" hosted in 2007 by the Center for Ethics and Values at the University of Alabama, Birmingham, is a hopeful sign that philosophy is beginning to enter the conversation about addiction.

[3]To date, only two theologians have published monographs on addiction: Linda Mercadante, *Victims and Sinners: Spiritual Roots of Addiction and Recovery* (Louisville: Westminster John Knox Press, 1996); and James Nelson, *Thirst: God and the Alcoholic Experience* (Louisville: Westminster John Knox Press, 2004). In addition, several Christian physicians and counselors have written on addiction. Most notable among these are *Addiction and Grace* (New York: HarperCollins, 1988) by neurologist Gerald May; and *Alcohol, Addiction, and Christian Ethics* (Cambridge: Cambridge University Press, 2006) by psychiatrist Christopher Cook.

and importance about addiction. Furthermore, the questions left un-answered by scientific research and medical treatment are precisely questions that call for philosophical and theological analysis.

Now is the opportune time to clarify how words like *addiction* and *alcoholism* will be used throughout the argument. In the contemporary idiom, one might be taken to mean any of three things by saying, for example, that *x* is an alcoholic: (1) *x* has alcoholism "in the genes" and is therefore an alcoholic whether she has ever had a drop of alcohol or not; (2) *x* is a practicing alcoholic, exhibiting the standard marks of alcoholic drinking and behavior; or (3) *x* is a recovering alcoholic, but *x* is nevertheless still an alcoholic because she is especially susceptible to relapse, her brain chemistry has been permanently changed, and so on. Unless otherwise stated, I mean to pick out only (2) when I speak of addiction or alcoholism. We are interested in addictive *behavior,* and although broadening the definition may be at times therapeuti-cally or rhetorically useful, it raises the very questions with which this inquiry is especially concerned. If addictive behavior could be ex-plained without remainder in the language of science, then perhaps such broadened definitions could be justified. However, I shall argue that addictive behavior cannot be reductively explained in this way.

DEFINING ADDICTION NEUROLOGICALLY

The Institute of Medicine defines addiction as a "brain disease" characterized by "compulsive use of a drug."[4] The National Institute on Drug Abuse defines addiction as a "chronic, relapsing, brain dis-ease expressed in the form of compulsive behaviors."[5] The American Medical Association and the American Psychological Association have adopted similar definitions.[6]

---

[4]Institute of Medicine, *Dispelling the Myths About Addiction: Strategies to Increase Understanding and Strengthen Research* (Washington, D.C.: National Academy Press, 1997), p. 13.
[5]National Institute on Drug Abuse, "Addiction Science: From Molecules to Managed Care," www.nida.nih.gov/pubs/teaching/Teaching6/Teaching1.html.
[6]The term "substance dependence" is used interchangeably with "addiction" by each of these classification systems.

The logic on which federal health institutes and professional organizations base such definitions is surprisingly straightforward: "Drug addiction is a *brain disease* because the abuse of drugs leads to changes in the structure and function of the brain."[7] Specifically, it is argued, addiction is always accompanied by the related neurological adaptations of "tolerance" and "withdrawal." Tolerance is defined as a neurological process in which repeated doses of a drug over time elicit a progressively decreasing effect, causing a person to require higher or more frequent doses of the drug to achieve similar results. Withdrawal is defined as the dysphoria resulting from cessation or curbing of the use of the drug, involving the body's agitation at the disruption of the modified equilibriums it has established through the process of use.[8]

Typically, in seeking to offer definitions, we try to specify necessary and sufficient conditions for the object or phenomenon that is to be defined. Thus, for example, a circle could be defined as a closed plane curve in which all points on the curve are equidistant from a point within it called the center. To say that this definition provides necessary and sufficient conditions for "circle" is to say that for anything to be a circle it *must* meet these specifications (these specifications are necessary) and that meeting these specifications is *enough* to justify us calling something a circle (these specifications are sufficient). Therefore, if the neurological phenomena of tolerance and withdrawal are to ground the definition of addiction as a brain disease, two entailments must hold. First, it must be the case that the existence of an addiction entails the presence of tolerance and withdrawal (tolerance and withdrawal are necessary conditions for addiction). Second, it must be the case that the presence of tolerance and withdrawal entails the existence of an addiction (tolerance and

---

[7] National Institute on Drug Abuse, "NIDA InfoFacts: Understanding Drug Abuse and Addiction," www.nida.nih.gov/infofacts/understand.html. Emphasis in original.
[8] Institute of Medicine, *Dispelling the Myths*, p. 13.

withdrawal are sufficient conditions for addiction). Do these entailments hold?

Two basic objections stand in the way of an affirmative answer. On the one hand, tolerance and withdrawal occur to countless persons whom we would not consider addicted. For example, surgery patients who are given morphine or some other pain reliever often develop tolerance and withdrawal symptoms from the medication, but few of them become addicted. Most of them stop using the medication straightway at the prescribed time, despite the experience of withdrawal symptoms. On the other hand, many people whom we would consider addicted experience little or no tolerance or withdrawal symptoms from their addiction. For example, many U.S. soldiers reported being addicted to heroin during their tours in the Vietnam War, but the majority of them stopped using on return, reporting no withdrawal symptoms.[9] Tolerance and withdrawal symptoms, therefore, cannot be considered either necessary or sufficient conditions for addiction. Tolerance and withdrawal are by no means insignificant features of addiction. However, they are not definitive or constitutive of addiction.

To illustrate the point, consider the following hypothetical but plausible scenario. Two physiologically similar persons are exposed to similar amounts of morphine over a similar time period. One spends a month in the hospital on morphine, the other spends a month regularly experimenting with heroin (processed morphine). Suppose that, at the end of the month, both are subject to identical levels of tolerance and withdrawal. Suppose further that, upon release from the hospital, the first person promptly stops using morphine. The experimenter with heroin does not stop taking heroin, however, and claims to be addicted. What is the difference between

---

[9]This phenomenon has been demonstrated in a number of separate studies. See Mark Keller, "On Defining Alcoholism: With Comment on Some Other Relevant Words," in *Alcohol, Science, and Society Revisited*, ed. Lisansky Gomberg, Helene Raskin White and John A. Carpenter (Ann Arbor: University of Michigan Press, 1982), pp. 119-33.

the two? Whatever the difference, it cannot be a simple matter of tolerance and withdrawal.

At this point, the defender of the disease concept of addiction may hunker down. We can imagine the response: "All of this business about necessary and sufficient conditions is a red herring. Our argument is really quite simple. Drug abuse leads to changes in the structure and function of the brain. Changes in behavior that can be traced to changes in brain structure and function are involuntary. Therefore, the behavior of persons with addictions is involuntary. And therefore, addiction is more akin to a human disease than a type of human action."

This is indeed a simple argument, but is it sound? It looks valid, so we must ask if its premises are true. The first premise seems beyond dispute: ample studies demonstrate that the abuse of drugs changes the structure and function of the brain. The problem with the argument comes in the second premise, which claims that changes in behavior that can be traced to changes in brain structure and function are involuntary. The premise is problematic because, if it were true, it would turn out that all sorts of activities that we consider voluntary are in fact involuntary. For instance, studies show that the brain structure and function of skilled musicians are transformed by years of practice. But surely this does not entail that, at some point, skilled musicians cease to be voluntarily engaged in playing their instruments. Surely it does not entail that playing the cello may cease to be something a cellist does and becomes something a cellist suffers, a kind of disease.

The second premise is therefore false. From the fact that a behavior can be correlated with changed brain structure and function, we cannot infer that the behavior in question is involuntary. We must ask a different sort of question in order to make that determination.

ASSESSING RISK GENETICALLY

If the difference between the addicted and the nonaddicted person cannot be rigorously specified in terms of brain chemistry, perhaps it can be specified in terms of some other physiological characteristic. In recent years, with rapid advances in genetics, researchers have suggested that the difference between addicted and nonaddicted persons might be explained by differences in genetic makeup. They claim that some persons are genetically predisposed to certain kinds of addiction.

Early advances in the genetics of addiction were the result of studies of the difference in alcoholism rates between fraternal and identical twins. In general, identical twins had more similar rates of alcoholism than did fraternal twins although there was nothing approaching an exact correspondence. In an effort to control for environmental factors, studies were then conducted on adopted children who were separated at birth from their biological parents. In general, adoptees that had at least one alcoholic biological parent were found more likely to be alcoholic than adoptees who did not have an alcoholic biological parent. In one study, the rate of alcoholism in the former group was four times that of the rate of alcoholism in the latter.[10]

More recently, geneticists have succeeded in isolating genes specifically related to certain substance addictions. So, for example, a 2005 study reported that a particular variation of the mu-opioid receptor gene led to increased sensitivity to the effects of addictive substances and therefore to higher risk of addiction.[11] Other studies have demonstrated that a variant of the alcohol dehydrogenase (ADH) gene increases the risk of alcoholism and that this particular variant is more prominent in persons of European descent.[12] Similar

[10]See Donald Goodwin, *Alcoholism: The Facts*, 3rd ed. (Oxford: Oxford University Press, 2000), chap. 13, for a summary of this and several other studies, as well as a general synopsis of findings relating alcoholism to heredity.

[11]Ying Zhang, Danxin Wang, Andrew D. Johnson, Audrey C. Papp and Wolfgang Sadee, "Allelic Expression Imbalance of Human Mu Opioid Receptor (OPRM1) Caused by Variant A118G," *Journal of Biological Chemistry* 280 (2005): 32618-24.

[12]John I. Nurnberger Jr. and Laura Jean Bierut, "Seeking the Connections: Alcoholism and Our Genes," *Scientific American*, April 2007, pp. 46-53.

studies are being conducted in genetics laboratories around the world, and new findings are made public on a regular basis.[13]

However, when we examine the proposed connection between these genes and increased risk for substance addictions, we run into a familiar problem. The connection has to do primarily with three factors. Persons who have these genes exhibit a more immediate and powerful attraction to the relevant drug on use, and/or develop tolerance to the drug more quickly and severely, and/or experience more acute withdrawal symptoms in the absence of the drug. We have already established that the occurrence of tolerance and withdrawal does not constitute either a necessary or sufficient condition for addiction, and the same can be said for the occurrence of the intense hedonic or antidysphoric experience of a drug. Many persons experience intense sensory gratification from using a drug but nevertheless do not become addicted. Indeed, such an intense experience may provide powerful reasons never to use the drug again, let alone become addicted to it.

With respect to each of these factors, whether or not a person becomes addicted seems to depend not simply on the experiences of gratification, tolerance or withdrawal, but rather on the significance that the person discerns or invests in those experiences. That is to say, experiences of gratification, tolerance or withdrawal do not directly *cause* addictive behavior but rather enter in to an agent's appraisal of whether or not to engage in addictive behavior. This is why genetic research could never provide a sufficient causal account of addiction. Thus the following optimistic conclusion of Donald Goodwin on the matter is unwarranted: "The ultimate jackpot in alcoholism research would be the identification of a single gene or group of genes that influences drinking behavior. . . . When an 'al-

---

[13]For an up-to-date log of the most important findings, as well as a measured assessment of the relevance of these findings to addiction research and therapies, see the webpage of the Genetic Science Learning Center at the University of Utah: http://learn.genetics.utah.edu/units/addiction/genetics.

cogene' has finally been identified, if ever, it may turn out that a single gene determines whether a person is alcoholic or non-alcoholic."[14]

It could never turn out that a single gene or group of genes determines whether a person is alcoholic because genes do not determine persons, as Goodwin's own studies of alcoholism rates in identical twins should have made clear. If genes *determined* addiction, then every person with the ADH1 variant of the alcohol dehydrogenase gene would become an alcoholic, which is of course not the case. Many genetic researchers openly acknowledge this and implore the general public to recognize the limitations of their research. As Wolfgang Sadee, one author of the study on the mu-opioid receptor gene, points out: "Regardless of what gene variant someone has, everyone has the potential to become addicted. So it is not that some people will be completely protected against addiction. . . . This finding just points to one of the factors that control susceptibility."[15]

There is a fundamental flaw in the argument that moves from genetic predisposition for addiction to disease attribution—a flaw that parallels the one discovered in the inference from changed brain chemistry to involuntary behavior. For this argument depends on a similar assumption, namely that if an activity is influenced by genes it is therefore involuntary. Yet this assumption is routinely rejected as we analyze the influence of genes on other everyday activities. With the completion of the human genome project, hardly a week passes without the discovery of a new gene that correlates in one way or another with patterns of human behavior. We are now aware that our genes play a role in everything from how cheerful we are to whether or not we are religious. Despite their efforts to the contrary, children often end up thinking and acting very much like their par-

---

[14]Goodwin, *Alcoholism*, p. 86.

[15]A summary of the study, as well as these comments by Sadee, can be found in Eva Gladek, "Addiction Gene," on the Sciencentral webpage: www.sciencentral.com/articles/view.php3 ?article_id=218392744&cat=1_1.

ents do, and this is partly a function of the way in which our genes influence our thinking and acting. And yet, we are not inclined to think that cheerful demeanors or religious observance are diseases. Why, then, should we conclude that addiction is a disease simply because addiction has genetic underpinnings? Unless we are content to reduce *all* human behavior to pathology, we must reject the assumption that genetic influence entails biological determinism.

TREATING ADDICTION MEDICALLY

Neither neural adaptations brought on by substance abuse nor a genetic predisposition for addiction provides sufficient evidence that addiction is a disease. But perhaps an argument for reducing addiction to biology can be grounded on the fact that addictions can be treated medically. If science affords the only or even the best hope for "treating" addiction, then perhaps addiction is best understood as a disease. And if, barring medical treatment, relapse into addictive behavior is guaranteed or even highly likely, then perhaps there is empirical justification for speaking of persons with addictions as biologically *compelled* to practice their addictions.

The disease concept of addiction maintains, first, that addiction is a chronic physiological disorder, and second, that it therefore can be most adequately treated through medical intervention. As it turns out, however, neither of these claims is supported by the evidence. In fact, contrary to the prevailing view of addiction, most substance abusers *do* stop practicing their addictions and go on to lead lives free of addiction, without relapse. Furthermore, the great majority of these addicted persons recover in a nonmedicalized context.

"Once an addict, always an addict" is a recurrent platitude among addicted persons and addiction experts alike.[16] And, interestingly, there seems to be evidence for this view *among those addicted persons*

---

[16] Alcoholics Anonymous World Services, *Alcoholics Anonymous*, 4th ed. (New York: Alcoholics Anonymous World Services, 2001), p. 33. Hereafter, *Alcoholics Anonymous* will be abbreviated AA and cited in-text.

who seek medicalized treatment: "In fact, most alcohol- and drug-dependent patients relapse *following cessation of treatment.* . . . In general about 50-60% of patients begin re-using within six months *following treatment cessation,* regardless of the type of discharge, the patient characteristics or the particular substance(s) of abuse."[17] And yet, most persons who meet the criteria for addiction have never been in *treatment* and therefore fall outside the scope of these studies.

What do we find about relapse within the general population of persons with addictions? Several large national surveys over the last thirty years have established that addiction is not a chronic disorder. Using the criteria for addiction provided by such organizations as the American Psychological Association and the National Institute on Alcohol Abuse and Alcoholism, these national surveys registered (a) the percentage of the population who had, at some time in their lives, met the criteria for substance dependence, and (b) the percentage of the population who reported no drug-related problems for at least twelve months prior to the survey. Comparing the two numbers allows us to establish the percentage of the general population who were once engaged in addictive behavior but have since ceased such behavior. This gives us a sense of the "rate of remission" of addiction. Given the prevailing view in addiction research, the numbers are bewildering. The Epidemiologic Catchment Area Study of 1980-1984 placed the "remission rate" for addiction at 59 percent; the National Comorbidity Survey of 1990-1992 at 74 percent; the National Epidemiologic Survey on Alcohol and Related Conditions of 2001-2003 at 81 percent; and the National Comorbidity Survey of 2001-2003 at 82 percent.[18]

Not only do the results of these surveys undermine the thesis that addiction is a disease characterized by chronic relapse, but also these

---

[17]A. Thomas McLellan, quoted in Gene Heyman, *Addiction: A Disorder of Choice* (Cambridge, Mass.: Harvard University Press, 2009), p. 66. Emphasis mine.

[18]The details of each of these surveys, analysis of the methods employed and interpretation of the results is provided in Heyman, *Addiction*, chap. 4.

surveys undermine the thesis that medicalized treatment is the only or even the best means of recovery. The numbers suggest just the opposite of what we would expect given a biologically reductive definition of addiction. Remission rates for addicts in treatment hover somewhere between 10 and 40 percent, significantly worse than the remission rates reported of the general population, most of whom do not seek treatment.[19]

Two comments about these findings are in order. First, they explain why researchers and clinicians have formulated an understanding of addiction that is at odds with the most comprehensive evidence: addiction researchers have drawn their conclusions based largely on studies involving addicted persons who are in medical treatment programs, ignoring the significantly larger population of addicted persons who never seek treatment. Second, the numbers *cannot* be used to support the thesis that medical treatment of addiction is deleterious or inferior. This is because of a bias in medical research known as "Birkson's bias." Birkson's bias refers to the fact that patients who seek treatment for a particular disorder are more likely than other patients to exhibit comorbidity—that is, to suffer from other disorders in addition to the disorder in question.[20] Thus it is just as likely that the lower remission rates among addicted persons who are in treatment are due to the difficulties that comorbidity poses to recovery rather than to some deficiency intrinsic to medicalized treatment of addiction.

Nevertheless, the best evidence would suggest that a biological definition of addiction as disease cannot be grounded in the success of medical treatment. Most persons with addictions recover in non-medicalized contexts, and furthermore, there is no evidence to suggest that medical treatment improves the chances of recovery from addiction.

Some proponents of the disease paradigm propose that effective

---

[19]Ibid., p. 66.
[20]Ibid., pp. 67-68.

treatment without medical intervention does not rule out the possibility of disease. For example, George Vaillant argues that "effective treatment of early coronary heart 'disease' probably depends far more upon changing bad habits than upon receiving medical treatment," yet we do not thereby rule out calling such a condition a "disease."[21]

Vaillant is correct to point out the elasticity of the concept of disease. We must take these types of arguments on a case-by-case basis. In this case, the salient difference between alcoholism and heart disease is that the central symptom of alcoholism is the inability to abstain from alcohol whereas none of the central symptoms of heart disease implicate human choice. If addiction were a disease, it would be a disease that presents the deterioration of the human power of choice as its primary symptom. There are diseases that attack human cognitive and conative powers—Alzheimer's comes to mind. But with Alzheimer's, the only hope of recovery is pharmacological, which is not true of addiction. Indeed, if the defining symptom of a condition is a bad habit that requires amendment, one wonders why the condition should be called a disease instead of a bad habit.

SCIENCE, PHILOSOPHY AND THEOLOGY

Despite the failure of the addiction research establishment to evidentially ground its assessment of addiction as disease, in the wider population, the media and even many in the medical establishment, the belief that science is approaching an ultimate panacea for addiction persists. So, for example, Dr. Matthew Torrington claims, "With the scientific advances we're making in understanding how the human brain works there's no reason we can't eradicate addiction in the next 20 or 30 years. We can do it by fixing the part of the brain that turns on you during drug addiction and encourages you to kill yourself against your will. I think addiction is the most beatable

---

[21]George Vaillant, *The Natural History of Alcoholism Revisited* (Cambridge, Mass.: Harvard University Press, 1995), p. 18.

of all the major problems we face. And I think we will."[22]

Although this is an extreme and probably unrepresentative viewpoint within the medical community, it does bring to the surface exactly what is at stake in any scientifically reductive account of addiction. Such reductive accounts of addiction assume a direct and therefore deterministic causal relationship between brain structure and behavior. This is the mistake that has emerged recurrently in the reasoning that buttresses the disease concept of addiction. From the recognition that certain behaviors are the result of changes in the brain, supporters of the disease concept of addiction illicitly infer that such behaviors are therefore involuntary. I have shown that, in order to determine whether a behavior is voluntary or involuntary, we must ask different questions than those being pursued by proponents of the disease concept of addiction. Drawing a line between the voluntary and the involuntary requires philosophical analysis.

Given our penchant for what C. S. Lewis terms "chronological snobbery," it may seem initially odd to return to ancient and medieval resources for help in untangling the complex question of how to distinguish between voluntary and involuntary human behavior, but that is what I propose to do. I turn in particular to the philosophical thought of Aristotle and Thomas Aquinas for help with this difficult question, for both of these thinkers were intensely interested in the relationship between the human body and human behavior.

Neither Aristotle nor Aquinas would have been especially surprised to learn of a "genetic predisposition" to certain types of human activity since this would only be a more specific statement of what they already believed to be the case, namely that human beings are born with bodily "natures" and that the body has a bearing on the way that humans feel, think and behave. Aristotle, for instance, had this to say about the biological transmission of behavioral traits: "Foolish, drunken, and harebrained women most often bring forth

---

[22]Quoted in Benoit Denizet-Lewis, "An Anti-Addiction Pill?" *The New York Times Magazine,* June 25, 2006.

children like unto themselves."[23] More precisely (and less chauvinistically), Aquinas states: "On the part of the body, in respect of the individual nature, there are some appetitive habits by way of natural beginnings. For some are disposed from their own bodily temperament to chastity or meekness or such like."[24]

For Aquinas, however, a natural predisposition to chastity or meekness does not thereby remove chaste or meek behavior from the realm of human action. Human action is circumscribed by the boundary between the voluntary and the involuntary. Voluntary action implies knowledge of an end and is epitomized by an agent's ability to give reasons for what she does. Because human beings have, in addition to their desires, the ability to form beliefs about what is suitable to them, they are able to act rather than merely be acted on. Thus, for instance, though a person may be predisposed to lust, that person is nevertheless able to *act* chastely in the face of temptation because she can recognize that lustfulness is not suitable to the end for which she strives. Conversely, though a person may be predisposed to chastity, that person is able to *act* lustfully because she may reason that lust serves her desired ends. Whenever movement is connected with rationality it becomes action.

The basic insight offered by Aquinas here is that we cannot determine whether human behavior is voluntary by examining bodily constitutions, whether genetic or neuronal. That is because genetic predispositions and brain configuration influence *both* voluntary *and* involuntary behaviors, as the arguments of this chapter have shown. Both the voluntary finger-picking of the master guitarist and the involuntary tics of the Tourette's victim are correlated with specific

---

[23]Quoted in *Autobiographical Writing Across the Disciplines,* ed. Diane P. Freeman and Olivia Frey (Durham, N.C.: Duke University Press, 2003), p. 320. I have not been able to locate this passage in Aristotle's writings.

[24]St. Thomas Aquinas, *Summa Theologica,* trans. Fathers of the English Dominican Province (Notre Dame, Ind.: Ave Maria Press, 1981), 1-2.51.1. Hereafter, all citations from the *Summa Theologica* will be supplied in-text. Thus, 1-2.51.1 denotes *Summa Theologica,* First Part of the Second Part *(Prima Secundae),* Question 51, Article 1.

developments in brain structure and function. This is why scientific efforts to defend the disease concept of addiction with sole reference to genetic or neurological features not only *have* failed but indeed are *bound* to fail.

If we wish to determine whether or not a certain sort of human behavior is voluntary, we must look elsewhere. Where shall we look? Aquinas's answer is straightforward. We have to ask whether or not the behavior in question is directed to certain ends; that is, we have to ask whether or not the behavior in question is sensitive to reason. This turns out to be a deep and difficult philosophical question because reason can be tied to action in complicated and paradoxical ways. For example, it is hard to understand how it is possible that we voluntarily act to what we know to be our own detriment, and yet we sometimes say that we did something even though we knew it would be bad for us. Addicted persons often talk this way about their behavior. A long and venerable philosophical tradition has wrestled with the complex and perplexing connections between reason and action. Exploring this tradition can help us better understand the nature of addictive behavior.

2

ADDICTION
AND INCONTINENCE

RESOURCES IN ARISTOTLE

◆

Should addiction be understood as a disease or as a choice? This is the most longstanding and contentious question in addiction research. The question, however, rests on a false dichotomy. The false dichotomy arises from a failure or an inability to conceive of a genuine space between compulsion and choice, between, in philosophical terms, determinism and voluntarism. This is a failure of philosophical memory, for indeed most moral philosophy until the modern era was concerned precisely with opening up and exploring the terrain between the determined involuntary and the spontaneous, unconstrained voluntary. The philosophical category that covers this terrain is the category of habit. I am convinced that if we are to avoid the false dichotomy that forestalls fresh thinking about addiction, we must recover the abandoned category of habit. To this end, I turn to the two great theorists of the terrain of habit, Aristotle and Thomas Aquinas, in order to make room conceptually for more sophisticated and adequate ways of thinking about addictive behavior.

THE PARADOX OF ADDICTION

According to the "Big Book" of Alcoholics Anonymous, alcoholism

is "cunning, baffling, [and] powerful" (AA 58). Alcoholism is said
to be "baffling" because of the "utter inability" of alcoholics to leave
alcohol alone, "no matter how great the necessity or the wish" (AA
34): "The fact is that most alcoholics, for reasons yet obscure, have
lost the power of choice in drink. Our so-called will power becomes
practically nonexistent. . . . We are without defense against the first
drink" (AA 24). The tyranny that alcohol seems to exercise over the
alcoholic's "power of choice" and "so-called will power" makes alcoholism "cunning" and "powerful."

However, according to Alcoholics Anonymous (hereafter A.A.),
this admission of powerlessness over alcohol is supposed to be the
"first step" toward regaining, in some sense, a power over alcohol:
"The principle that we shall find no enduring strength until we first
admit complete defeat is the main taproot from which our whole
Society has sprung and flowered."[1] The paradox of alcoholism is
that alcoholics acknowledge the futility of their own willpower to
resist alcohol, yet in a nonmedicalized program of recovery they find
access to a power sufficient to reinvigorate the once-impotent will.
Given that A.A.'s twelve-step program of recovery has been successfully adapted to treat a broad range of addictions, we can generalize
and characterize this as the paradox of addiction. Addicted persons
claim to be powerless over their addictive behavior, yet this admission itself is the inroad to regaining power over that same behavior.

In attempting to provide a response to this paradox, most addiction experts fall into one of two camps. The first focuses almost
exclusively on the near-unanimous claim of addicted persons that
their willpower or power of choice was insufficient to resist the allure of an addictive substance. This response accepts as paradigmatic
and literal such accounts of addiction as the following:

A man who, while under treatment for inebriety, during four weeks

---

[1]Alcoholics Anonymous World Services, *Twelve Steps and Twelve Traditions* (New York: Alcoholics Anonymous World Services, 1952), p. 22. Hereafter, *Twelve Steps and Twelve Traditions*
will be abbreviated TT and cited in-text.

secretly drank the alcohol from six jars containing morbid specimens. On asking him why he committed this loathsome act, he replied, "Sir, it is as impossible for me to control this diseased appetite as it is for me to control the pulsations of my heart."[2]

Were a keg of rum in one corner of the room, and were a cannon constantly discharging balls between me and it, I could not refrain from passing before that cannon, in order to get at the rum.[3]

In an effort to find an explanation for the impotence of the addictive will, the first response concurs with these addicted persons' self-descriptions and labels addiction a disease, locating the source of the addicted person's inability to stop using entirely outside of the will. According to this view, the material configuration of the disease, whether it be specified as neurological, genetic or cellular, overpowers the addicted person's will in such a way that he does not act voluntarily when he uses but is rather compelled to use.

The second response to the paradox of addiction focuses almost exclusively on the de facto ability of some persons to recover from addiction without medical intervention. Insofar as recovery involves the voluntary cessation of the addictive behavior, the addicted person's behavior prior to recovery is considered equally voluntary. The failure of willpower on the part of the addicted person is construed as a standard case of willful misconduct akin to other actions that involve the capitulation of the will in the face of temptation. What is at work in addiction, this view suggests, is not that a disease vitiates human willpower, but rather that, due to some kind of moral weakness, the addicted person repeatedly makes a deliberate decision to use. If the addicted person does not recover, it is only because he does not really want to. According to this view, "addiction is a choice."[4]

---

[2]William James, *The Principles of Psychology* (New York: Dover, 1950), 2:543.
[3]This is Benjamin Rush's quotation of one eighteenth-century drunkard, cited in Harry Gene Levine, "The Discovery of Addiction," *Journal of Studies on Alcohol* 39 (1978): 152.
[4]This is the title of a popular book written by psychologist Jeffrey A. Schaler: *Addiction Is a*

Neither response to the central paradox of addiction is adequate. The disease concept of addiction is unable to provide a coherent account of the obvious occurrence of recovery from addiction without the aid of medical intervention. By insisting on the language of determinism, the disease model is unable to enter into the conversation about the way in which the willpower of the addicted person is deconstructed and reconstituted through a nonmedical process of recovery. The notion of disease, with its corresponding suggestion of a physiologically determined compulsion to drink, cannot explain the alcoholic's failure to resist alcohol, for in doing so it would also predict that alcoholics are incapable of recovering without medical intervention, which is evidently not the case.

The confusion produced by the disease concept of addiction is more than merely conceptual. We live in a society in which billions of dollars are poured into the medical treatment of a disease called addiction at the same time that billions of dollars are spent to arrest and imprison persons for exhibiting the symptoms of the disease. As Gene Heyman points out, "we typically do not advocate incarceration and medical care for the same activities."[5] Relatedly, the confusion over addiction reinforces class stereotypes. The disease concept of addiction is routinely applied to wealthy addicts while the general public persists in thinking of poor addicts as morally depraved. Prison demographics suggest that the hypocrisy is reproduced in public policy.

The choice concept of addiction is equally inadequate to deal with the paradox of addiction and recovery, for different reasons.

Choice (Chicago: Open Court, 2000). The general line of argument has been reproduced in a number of books, including *The Useful Lie* (Wheaton, Ill.: Crossway, 1991) by Christian counselor William Playfair. The most prominent critic of the disease model is probably Stanton Peele. Athough Peele's approach is more subtle than the simplistic "addiction as choice" view, his attempts to articulate the nature of addiction often collapse back into voluntarism for lack of a robust philosophical alternative to disease or choice. See, e.g., *The Diseasing of America: How We Allowed Recovery Zealots and the Treatment Industry to Convince Us We Are Out of Control* (San Francisco: Jossey-Bass, 1995).

[5]Gene Heyman, *Addiction: A Disorder of Choice* (Cambridge, Mass.: Harvard University Press, 2009), p. 1.

Simply put, it makes intelligible the possibility of recovery only by denying the category of addiction. By insisting on the language of voluntarism, the choice model reduces addiction to mere weakness of will with respect to one substance or activity. In its more cynical mode, the choice model characterizes attributions of "addiction" as a perverse psychological form of rationalization and excuse. Defenders of the choice concept of addiction never tire of alleging that the disease paradigm excuses addicted persons from expending the effort to overcome addiction. The assumption behind the allegation is that excuses are what stand between an addict and recovery. Addiction is therefore not qualitatively distinct from any other failure of willpower; some people give in to the temptation for an extra piece of chocolate cake, others to the temptation to drink themselves to death.

The overwhelming report of alcoholics and other persons with serious addictions flies in the face of this attempt to reduce addictive behavior to a type of weakness of will that is perhaps greater in degree but not categorically distinct from other failures of the will. As addicted persons interpret and describe their addictive thought and behavior, they testify that the pull of addiction is qualitatively distinct from any other kind of strong temptation. This is, *functionally*, why the disease model of addiction has been helpful to many persons with addictions. It resonates with the addicted person's experience as something phenomenologically other than everyday struggles of will, thus removing the moral stigma that accompanies the choice concept of addiction, according to which addiction is simply willful misconduct. As Francis Seeburger puts it, "If nothing else, the spread of the disease view of addiction has greatly helped to overcome the illusion that addicts as a group are significantly different from other people when it comes to matters of ethics and morality."[6]

---

[6]Francis Seeburger, *Addiction and Responsibility: An Inquiry into the Addictive Mind* (New York: Crossroad, 1993), p. 68.

Persons with addictions describe their experiences in ways that do not easily fit with either the disease or the choice model of addiction. On the face of it, many of these descriptions appear to be downright contradictory. Perhaps the descriptions that addicted persons offer of their experiences are incoherent and there is no philosophical formulation of the range of human action that makes intelligible these types of descriptions. The burden of this and the next chapter will be to show, on the contrary, that addicted persons' interpretations and descriptions of their experience can be made philosophically intelligible, without reducing addiction to disease at one extreme or willful choice at the other.

If addiction is neither a disease nor a choice, what is it? This is the question that I have set for myself, yet it is not entirely clear that this is an intelligible question. After all, there is no such thing as addiction *simpliciter.* There are many different kinds of addictions. One common distinction is that between "substance" and "process" addictions. Substance addictions include addictions to chemicals such as alcohol, nicotine, amphetamines and opiates. Process addictions include addictions to particular behaviors such as viewing pornography, shopping, gambling and surfing the Internet. Moreover, there seem to be different degrees of addiction: we speak of people "becoming addicted," "struggling with an addiction," "being addicted" and "being severely addicted." Addictions come in all types and sizes. How, then, can I pose the straightforward question: "What is addiction?"

And yet, surely we mean to pick out something that all of these types of behavior share in common when we speak of them as "addictions." Unless there is some phenomenological "core" of the addictive experience, anything that might be said about addiction per se will die the death of a thousand qualifications, and the question "What is addiction?" will be meaningless. Moreover, unless at least some part of that phenomenological core of the addictive experience is perplexing and opaque to straightforward explanation, the question "What is addiction?" will be uninteresting. I propose that the question is meaningful. There are, indeed, experiences shared in common by most persons with addictions. I propose also that the question is interesting. Among the set of experiences shared in common by most addicted persons, some are extremely perplexing. When I ask, "What is addiction?" I am asking whether we can make sense of the most vexing aspects of addictive behavior that are shared in common by a wide range of addicted persons.

To begin to narrow our focus, therefore, we must attempt to locate addictive experience within a broad spectrum of descriptions of human action. I turn to Aristotle for help with this task, because Aristotle's philosophy of human action is sensitive to those subtle features of human action that demand precise distinctions and differentiations.

ADDICTION AND INCONTINENCE

At the broadest level, Aristotle distinguishes between four types of human action: virtuous action, continent action, incontinent action and vicious action. A virtuous action is performed whenever a person rationally approves of what is good, desires what is good and accordingly does what is good. A continent action is performed whenever a person rationally approves of what is good, desires what is bad, yet following reason, does what is good. An incontinent action is performed whenever a person rationally approves of what is good, desires what is bad, and following appetite, does what is bad. Finally, a vicious action is performed whenever a person rationally approves of what is bad (i.e., believes it to be good), desires the bad and accordingly does what is bad.

To call an action or a type of action "good" is simply to affirm that it is a fitting component of a worthwhile way of life. To call an action or a type of action "bad" is to deny that it is fitting to a worthwhile way of life. Assuming that addiction is destructive rather than conducive to human flourishing, addictive behaviors are bad and are therefore either incontinent or vicious or beyond the scope of human action altogether. How would we distinguish between the three?

The incontinent addicted person would be one who (a) has the belief that the addictive behavior is bad for him and a corresponding desire not to engage in it, and who (b) has some capacity to resist the behavior, but who (c) nevertheless does engage in addictive behavior against his own better judgment. Obviously, there are addictive experiences that do *not* fit this description. Aristotle would have suggested two different types of addictive experience that would definitely fall outside the range of incontinence. First, an addicted person could lack (a) the belief that the behavior in question is bad for him and the corresponding desire to avoid the addictive behavior. The addicted person who engages in addictive behavior in the absence of (a) would be termed by Aristotle the "self-indulgent" addict, and his behavior would fall under the category of vicious action. The self-indulgent addicted person not only engages in addictive activity but also does so wholeheartedly, believing the activity to be a good worthy of pursuit and therefore fully desiring it. The self-indulgent addicted person does not give in to a temptation that is contrary to what he believes he ought to do. Rather, the self-indulgent addicted person believes that the addictive behavior is what he ought to do. There is no internal "tension" as the self-indulgent addicted person engages in addictive behavior, and therefore the addictive behavior is not susceptible to redress.[7] To modify an old folk-saying, if you don't think it's broke, you won't try to fix it.

On the other hand, Aristotle would have held that an addicted person could lack (b)—some capacity to resist the addictive behavior—and therefore not be rightly described as incontinent. The ad-

---

[7]Harry Frankfurt, in his classic essay "Freedom of the Will and the Concept of a Person," in *Free Will*, ed. Gary Watson, 2nd ed. (Oxford: Oxford University Press, 2003), p. 335, offers a description of what he calls the "willing addict" that closely parallels our Aristotelian notion of the self-indulgent addict. In Frankfurt's philosophical vernacular, the willing addict is one who experiences no conflict between his or her first-order and second-order desires. The willing addict wants the addictive object and wants to want it.

dicted person who engages in addictive behavior in the absence of (b) would be termed by Aristotle a "morbid" addict, and his behavior would fall outside the scope of human action altogether. The morbid person is one who cannot rationally guide his actions "as a result of disease (e.g., of epilepsy) or of madness" (1149a11). Epilepsy and madness are such that they temporarily or permanently render the human person entirely a patient, removing all agency. In both cases, the agency of the person is rendered ineffectual, thereby removing the agent's behavior from the category of human action altogether. The relationship of the morbid addicted person to addictive behavior is precisely the same as the relationship of an epileptic to seizures. If one's agency is ineffectual, then it is not within one's power to rectify one's behavior; therefore, one is not acting at all but rather being acted on.

It is tempting to hear in Aristotle's language of "disease" and "madness" resonances of the contemporary disease concept of addiction. There is, however, a decisive difference between what Aristotle means by the notion of a morbid character and what is meant in the field of addiction studies by the characterization of addiction as disease. For Aristotle, one whose behavior is the result of disease or madness is thereby removed entirely from the realm of responsibility for that behavior. And this, indeed, comports with our normal understanding of a disease as something that is biologically *determined*. The contemporary disease concept of addiction, however, fudges at this point, claiming that the diseased victim, although perhaps not culpable for his actions, is nevertheless responsible to rectify them.

To return to Aristotle's taxonomy, some addicted persons would be rightly classified as self-indulgent or morbid on Aristotle's terms. Indeed, many addicted persons go through a self-indulgent phase, buoyed by the fleeting conviction that the addiction can be maintained without any drastic detriment to health or well-being. On the other hand, some addicted persons clearly lack the capacity for change because their agency has been rendered impotent or insufficient by some natural inheritance. The largest class of individuals who could be accurately described in Aristotle's language as "morbid addicts" are persons with serious mental illness or mental disability.

Interestingly, A.A. is quite hesitant to place people in this category: "There are those, too, who suffer from grave emotional and mental disorders, but many of them do recover if they have the capacity to be honest" (AA 58). With respect to the "beggars, tramps, asylum inmates, prisoners, queers, plain crackpots, and fallen women" that many early A.A. groups resolved not to admit to membership, later A.A. wisdom found that "thousands of these sometimes frightening people were to make astonishing recoveries and become our greatest workers and intimate friends" (TT 140-41).

Aristotle is more liberal in his attributions of morbidity. For example, he remarks, "It is surprising if a man is defeated by and cannot resist pleasures or pains which most men can hold out against, when this is not due to heredity or disease, like the softness that is hereditary with the kings of the Scythians, or that which distinguishes the female sex from the male" (1150b12-16). It seems likely that Aristotle would have been willing to place a large number of addicted persons in the "morbid" category and therefore that Aristotle would have been sympathetic to characterizing many addictions as determined by heredity. What Aristotle would *not* have accepted is the simultaneous claim that hereditary addicts can be held responsible for their addictions and expected to recover in a nonmedicalized context. Aristotle is too consistent for this. Hereditary determinism removes both culpability and responsibility on Aristotle's account, as is clear from this and other passages. However, since we know that most addicted persons show a capacity for recovery, thereby demonstrating that their addictive behavior is remediable, most persons with addictions would be inappropriately described as "morbid" or "diseased."

There is nothing particularly perplexing about the behavior of either the self-indulgent or the morbid addicted person. The self-indulgent addicted person believes that he ought to engage in addictive action, wishes to engage in addictive action, and therefore engages in addictive action. No mystery arises there. With respect to the morbid addicted person, he is physically determined to behave as he does. No mystery arises there, either. It is the behavior and experience of the *incontinent* addict that is truly puzzling, and so when we ask the question "What is addiction?" we are searching for a way of appropriately describing and giving an account of incontinent addictive action. Indeed, incontinent action in general is deeply puzzling, and Aristotle's treatment of the problem of simple incontinence can be extended and deepened to probe the unique nature of addictive incontinence. For it is in his attempt to grapple with the mystery of incontinence that Aristotle hits on the category of habit as indispensible to any adequate account of the spectrum of human action.

SOURCES OF INCONTINENCE

Incontinence presents a philosophical paradox in its own right. It can be characterized straightforwardly as what takes place when an agent acts against his own better judgment. It is so patently obvious from firsthand experience that this sort of thing occurs that it may not be immediately apparent why this is paradoxical, but that it is so can be shown as follows. If, as is commonly held, agents act in such a way as to bring about what they believe to be, on the whole, to their greatest benefit, then how can it come about that an agent genuinely believes that one course of action is to his greatest benefit and yet chooses to take a contradictory course of action? How can an agent choose to do that which he believes to be inferior to another course of action that was open for him to take?

Because the category of incontinence is often thought of primarily as the domain of choice, it might seem that to portray addiction as a form of incontinence is to capitulate to the choice model of addiction. However, this is a misunderstanding of the category of incontinence. The determinative test of incontinent behavior is not whether or not the behavior was the outcome of deliberative choice but, rather, whether or not the behavior is susceptible to correction through some exercise of human agency. In other words, whether or not the behavior was chosen through the exertion of a spontaneous and arbitrarily free will matters not for the attribution of incontinence; all that is required for the attribution of incontinence is that the agent can be held responsible for correcting his behavior through the exercise (over time) of his power of agency.

This clarification is important because it helps us understand that attributions of incontinence need not imply that an agent is *culpable* for his behavior. Often, persons come to act incontinently through no fault of their own. For example, Aristotle points out that the roots of some incontinent behavior can be traced back to childhood habituation or the force of custom. We might think especially of the formative power of sexual trauma and victimization. Thus Aristotle distinguishes between "simple incontinence"—incontinence that is the product of decisions knowingly made by a competent moral agent—and other subcategories of incontinence. Only in cases of simple incontinence can the agent be considered fully *culpable* for his behavior. Nevertheless, even in cases in which an agent is in no sense culpable for coming to behave as he does, he may nevertheless be held *responsible* for amending his ways since he is "able to respond" to his situation through the exertion of agency. Regardless of *how* a person came to be incontinent (and therefore regardless of how *culpable* a person may be in his incontinence), incontinent action itself remains mysterious. For regardless of *how* an agent came to have desires that contradict with his reason, it is still perplexing that reason should not always win out. Once an agent *believes* or *knows* that a line of action is bad, why should he ever take it?

In his attempt to respond to the paradox of incontinent action in book seven of the *Nicomachean Ethics*, Aristotle begins, as he often does, by registering what others have said about the matter. He reports that Socrates responded to the paradox by denying that there was a paradox in the first place: "For *Socrates* was entirely opposed to the view in question, holding that there is no such thing as incontinence; no one, he said, when he judges acts against what he judges best—people act so only by reason of ignorance" (1145b25-28). Socrates' position, then, is that genuine incontinence does not occur, since in any case of apparent incontinence the agent does not possess the knowledge with which his behavior is in contradiction. We always act in accord with our "better judgment," according to Socrates, even though to others observing or to our own retrospective gaze it appears that we should or could have "known better." Whenever an addicted smoker, for instance, lights up another cigarette, at that moment at least he believes that lighting up is in his best interest and he is, by implication, ignorant of the fact that lighting up is not in his best interest. And, of course, we cannot be held accountable for actions performed in ignorance. Incontinent action, on Socrates' view, is simply ignorant action and therefore not a moral failure.

In accord with his methodology of "saving the appearances," Aristotle rejects the Socratic response to the problem of incontinence, saying, "this view plainly contradicts the observed facts" (1145b29-30). He therefore seeks to provide a philosophically coherent explanation of incontinent action that does not, in the process, simply deny the category of incontinent action altogether.

In the course of Aristotle's treatment of the puzzle of incontinence, two lines of response emerge. The first type of response Aristotle proposes is that, sometimes, the reasoning needed to overcome incontinent action is simply not completed due to the interruption of passion. The second type of response he proposes is that, sometimes, although the reasoning may be completed, it is not followed due to the weight of habit.

En route to offering his first response to the puzzle, Aristotle draws a distinction between what he calls "potential knowledge" and "actual knowledge": "It will make a difference whether, when a man does what he should not, he has the knowledge but is not exercising it, or *is* exercising it; for the latter seems strange, but not the former" (1136b32-35). A distinction can be made between a rational judgment possessed but not exercised and a rational judgment exercised; the former is potential, the latter actual, knowledge.

As he develops the significance of this distinction for the question of incontinence, Aristotle depends on an account of action according to which action can always be represented as the outcome of a practical syllogism. A practical syllogism consists of two premises, one universal and the other particular. The universal premise makes a universal judgment such as "Everything sweet ought to be tasted" (1147a29). The particular premise makes a particular judgment such as "This is sweet" (1147a29). When a valid connection is made between a universal and particular premise, an action is the culmination of the syllogism: The sweet thing is tasted. For Aristotle, then, every human act can be represented as the consequence of a practical syllogism. I say that every human act *can* be represented as the consequence of a practical syllogism to underscore the point that syllogistic reasoning need not precede every human action. Often, the construction of a practical syllogism is performed retrospectively to display or assess the rationality of a given action.

Based on his view of human action as the consequence of a practical syllogism, Aristotle explains how an agent can *in a sense* possess a judgment yet act contrary to that judgment. Since, on the account Aristotle has begun to develop, all human action can be represented as the consequence of a practical syllogism, it seems as though incontinent action will require that the agent possess, in some sense, two practical syllogisms—one that, had it been rightly connected in the agent's mind, would have led to a right action and another that *is* connected in the agent's mind and therefore *actually* leads to a wrong action. In every such case, the rational judgment that would have led to continent action is possessed by the agent, not actually, but merely potentially, at the moment the incontinent action is performed. Aristotle suggests a variety of ways in which this might occur.

First, the needed premise may be merely potentially known because of a lack of time. The agent may be rushed or rush to act before bringing the appropriate premise to mind. Second, the needed premise may be merely potentially known because strong appetite interrupts or distorts the deliberative process (1147a32-35). Third, the needed premise may be merely potentially known because a constitutional change (such as drunkenness) incapacitates the deliberative process (1147a14-18).

This concludes Aristotle's first line of response according to which incontinent action is possible because the reasoning that would be needed to prevent it, although accessible to the agent and therefore "potentially known," is not actually carried out at the crucial moment. Aristotle dubs the incontinence that results from this kind of failure "impetuous incontinence." Impetuous incontinence occurs whenever hurry, strong appetite or an abnormal bodily state wrecks the deliberative process that is needed to arrive at a right judgment, which would lead to a right action.

Aristotle's analysis of impetuous incontinence puts us in a position to better understand a wide range of addictive behaviors. First, the way in which bodily alteration can disrupt the deliberative process is on display in addicted persons' "within-episode" (e.g., after the first drink) "loss of control" over their addictive behavior. Second, the way in which bodily alteration can disrupt the deliberative process is on display when persons with addictions report that their behavior was due to intense "physical craving" for an addictive substance. And third, the way in which strong appetites can interrupt or distort the deliberative process is on display when addicted persons report that their behavior was due to "psychological craving" for an addictive substance. Let us take each of these in turn.

Although it is the centerpiece of the disease concept of addiction, the concept of "loss of control" is often not clearly specified. What exactly do, say, alcoholics lose control over: the ability to resist the first drink or the ability to stop drinking once they have taken the first drink? Donald Goodwin, a leading alcohol studies expert, contends that "loss of control refers to the alcoholic's inability to stop drinking once he starts."[8] This restriction, however, poses a dilemma on the standard disease view of alcoholism. For if loss of control is triggered only *after* the first drink, why should the alcoholic not simply be able to resist the first drink? In any event, given Aristotle's analysis of the role of constitutional change in impetuous incontinence, within-episode addictive behavior is not especially surprising. Given the way in which addictive behavior reconfigures the neurological structure of the addictive brain, the first drink or the first hit of a drug does indeed bring about a decisive constitutional change in the addicted person's body—a much more decisive change than that brought about when a nonaddicted person takes a first drink or a first hit of a drug. We are not surprised when drunk people generally fail to reason well about their behavior, and so within-episode "loss of control" by persons with addictions should not be surprising either. Within-episode addictive behavior is indeed the least mysterious type of addictive behavior, and the processes at work in it are accounted for by Aristotle's analysis of impetuous incontinence.

What about addictive behavior that is purported to be in response to craving? Craving is a complex concept, difficult to define, but a common albeit imprecise distinction between "physical craving" and "psychological craving" will help to elucidate it. Biologically, this distinction is finally untenable since *all* desire has a physiological correlate. Nevertheless, the distinction is useful because it maps onto certain of our phenomenological intuitions. Thus let us say that "physical craving" means that the agent can point to what ails (the head if it is a headache, the stomach if it is nausea, the hands if it is tremors, et cetera), whereas "psychological craving" means that what is disturbing the agent is not similarly locatable by the agent.

---

[8] Donald Goodwin, *Alcoholism: The Facts,* 3rd ed. (Oxford: Oxford University Press, 2000), p. 90.

Physical craving is the intense and persistent desire to engage in addictive behavior as a means of escape from bodily discomfort. Its characteristic symptoms can include cold sweats, nausea and uncontrollable shaking. These bodily experiences are often said to be consequences of physical withdrawal from an addictive substance, and the withdrawal resulting from the lack of the substance is said to be evidence of physical tolerance and dependence. Some addicted persons experience no physical craving, and some persons who experience physical craving are not addicted (recall the hospital patient on morphine). Nevertheless, physical craving often accompanies the experience of addiction.

Physical craving would seem to be a clear instance of the way in which strong desire can obstruct continent action because it is associated with what Aristotle called a constitutional change. How are we to understand human action in the face of strong visceral desire? We can imagine cases in which bodily discomforts cause desires, even strong desires, which are nevertheless quite easily resisted. Even a very thirsty person can resist the desire to drink from a stagnant pool of water that he knows to be infested with harmful bacteria, especially if there is reason to believe the thirst can be safely relieved at a later time. But we can push this example to the point where the power of choice seems to be in serious jeopardy. Simply removing the expectation that the thirst can be safely relieved in the near future pushes us in this direction, and it is not hard for us to imagine a thirst so intense that a normal person would drink what he knew to be harmful or even deadly water in the absence of a reasonable hope of future relief. In such a case, bodily need trumps the deliberative process.

A similar process occurs whenever addicted persons engage in behavior that they "know" to be harmful to them in response to intense bodily need. Take, for example, William Burroughs's explanation of why persons addicted to heroin seem unable to voluntarily resist taking heroin in the face of certain withdrawal symptoms: "The reason it is practically impossible to stop using and cure yourself is that the sickness lasts five to eight days. Twelve hours of it would be easy, twenty-four possible, but five to eight days is too long."[9] We can imagine a similar explanation of why a person stranded at sea would eventually be practically unable to resist drinking seawater, even if he "knew" it would kill him. There is, therefore, no great mystery to instances of addictive behavior that can be explained with reference to intense visceral desires. Such addictive behavior fits well into Aristotle's category of impetuous incontinence.

Not all craving, however, rises to the level of visceral need that would explain some kinds of addictive behavior. Many addicted persons must be literally locked up for some period of time upon cessation from their addictive activity since they are practically incapable of resisting their overwhelming visceral desires, but once physical craving has subsided, the addicted person must be released to fend for himself. This is not because the addicted person is free of craving. Rather, it is because the craving has ceased to be primarily physical and has become predominantly psychological. Can addictive behavior prompted by psychological craving also be fit into Aristotle's category of impetuous incontinence?

Generally, psychological craving is characterized by a mix of euphoric and dysphoric urges, desires to experience satisfaction and desires to be relieved of dissatisfaction. Even when it is not rooted in bodily need, desire can derail an agent's pursuit of continent action by making the agent over-consider a certain particular premise of practical reason at the cost of under-considering, and eventually not considering, the appropriate premise. The strong psychological desire for an object can distract or prevent the agent from considering the particular premise that he or she knows potentially but needs to exercise in order to act continently.

But when we put the matter this way, it is hard to see how the

---

[9]William Burroughs, *Junky* (New York: Penguin Books, 1977), p. 94.

"psychological craving" of addiction is any different than everyday experiences of temptation to indulgence faced by addicted and non-addicted persons alike. If failure with respect to these everyday experiences of temptation is to be understood straightforwardly as a failure of moral choice, then should we not also understand the addicted person's capitulation to psychological craving as a simple choice? After all, since the will exercises some power over the passions, we are not simply at the beck and call of our desires. Although desire often comes to us unbidden, as an event in our psychological lives, we are not without resources for dealing with it. We are capable of directing the intellect away from consideration of the occurrent desire. As human agents, it is within our power to voluntarily choose not to dwell on desires that intrude on us. Taken singly, then, there is never a case of "mere" psychological desire that we are unable to resist by redirecting the gaze of the intellect.

However, the psychological craving that accompanies addiction represents a special threat to our abilities to resist desire because the desires that constitute psychological craving never come singly. The desire of psychological craving is unlike any other type of desire, not in its intensity—which can vary widely—but rather in its resilience.[10] Addictive desires are indefatigably persistent. They intrude on the agent's consciousness not once or twice but repeatedly. Every effort to direct the gaze of the intellect away from the object of desire or to call the intellect to reflect on the inferiority of the object of desire is met, not by relief from the immediate threat, but rather by a new attacker in a similar guise. If the conflict between the will and non-addictive desire (e.g., the desire for one too many pieces of cake) is a battle, then the conflict between the will and addictive craving is a war of attrition. William Irvine asks, "Why does the will play second fiddle" to resilient desire in such wars?

---

[10]R. Jay Wallace, "Addiction as Defect of the Will: Some Philosophical Reflections," in *Free Will*, ed. Gary Watson (Oxford: Oxford University Press, 2003), makes much of the distinctively resilient nature of addictive desire.

For the simple reason that they [resilient desires] refuse to fight fairly. The emotions, in their dealings with the intellect, don't use reason to gain its cooperation. Instead they wear it down with—what else?—emotional entreaties. They beg, whine, and bully. They won't take no for an answer. They won't give the intellect a moment's peace. In most cases, the best the intellect can hope for is to withstand these entreaties for a spell. Then it succumbs.[11]

Gerald May puts the same point more succinctly: "Willpower and resolution come and go, but the addictive process never sleeps."[12] Psychological craving is the great enemy of continent action simply because it pits a force of seemingly inexhaustible resources against a limited power, the human will. As soon as one addictive desire is banished from the scene, another appears. Craving fires volley after volley of singular desires into an agent's consciousness, gradually exhausting the limited power of human will. Thus psychological craving can be a potent source of impetuous incontinence.

As we have seen, within-episode addictive behavior and addictive behavior that is triggered by intense physical or unremitting psychological craving can be understood as extreme exemplifications of impetuous incontinence. Indeed, as we recognize the fragile relationship between human willpower and strong visceral or unremitting psychological desire, a wide range of addictive behavior becomes intelligible.

Nevertheless, what is most perplexing about addictive behavior remains untouched by this analysis. For what is most perplexing about addictive behavior is that addicted persons regularly engage in addictive behavior *in the absence of* strong visceral or unremitting psychological craving. Both physical and psychological cravings are transitory states; we know from physiological studies and from the testimonies of persons with addictions that both kinds of craving

---

[11]William Irvine, *On Desire: Why We Want What We Want* (Oxford: Oxford University Press, 2006), p. 76.

[12]Gerald May, *Addiction and Grace* (New York: HarperCollins, 1988), p. 52.

diminish and may eventually disappear. The duration of *physical* craving is biologically circumscribed and therefore fairly uniform among persons addicted to the same substance. The duration of *psychological* craving is influenced by a wider range of factors and is therefore less uniform among addicted persons, nevertheless all addicts experience a movement from unremitting psychological craving to intermittent desire (which is often "cue dependent"). Many persons in recovery testify that they no longer crave the addictive substance at all.

Yet relapse often occurs even after the cessation of craving. How are we to account for this? We cannot account for it by drawing on the category of impetuous incontinence. We return, then, to Aristotle's broad treatment of incontinence, seeking resources to address this most perplexing of addictive behaviors. It is at this point that the category of habit emerges as the indispensable key to unlocking the most vexing aspects of addictive incontinence. For it is the category of habit that can explain how it is possible for an agent to both rationally determine that a behavior should be rejected and yet voluntarily engage in that behavior.

In contrast to cases of impetuous incontinence in which an agent is prevented from reaching the appropriate conclusion about his action, Aristotle says that sometimes an incontinent agent actually reaches the conclusion of the practical syllogism that should lead to continent action but nevertheless violates that conclusion. For example, Aristotle claims that "the incontinent man acts with appetite, but not with choice; while the continent man on the contrary acts with choice, but not with appetite" (1111b12-15). At numerous places throughout the *Nicomachean Ethics*, Aristotle makes the same claim: The incontinent agent is sometimes one who acts contrary to his choice or rational judgment.

This is a strange saying to our ears. How could an agent act against his own choice? Isn't an agent's choice always made evident by what the agent actually does? Not so for Aristotle. But how, then, does Aristotle believe that an agent could act contrary to the judgment delivered by right practical reasoning? Aristotle thinks this is possible because of the role of habit in human action: "The fact that men use the language that flows from knowledge proves nothing; for . . . those who have just begun to learn a science can string together its phrases, but do not yet know it; for it has to become part of themselves, and that takes time" (1147a19-23).

Here, Aristotle connects incontinent action with habit, which he defines elsewhere as a kind of second nature (1152a31). The passage sheds light on how an agent might indeed possess the rational judgment that follows from a practical syllogism and yet act contrary to that judgment. The agent might "have" the conclusion in a sense, yet fail to act on it because it has not "become a part" of himself; it has not become "second nature" to him. What seems to be lacking in this type of case is the incorporation of knowledge into action. Insofar as habit is a kind of embodied knowledge (a definition that seems apt given Aristotle's description of habit as "second nature"), then in certain cases what interferes with the incontinent agent's ability to act in accordance with his choice is a wrong habit or at least the lack of a right habit. As Risto Saarinen explains, some incontinent people "are like inexperienced youngsters who cannot yet profit from their knowledge, because they lack the proper habits. It is not the lack of knowledge but the lack of a proper integration of that knowledge which causes the right choice not to be followed."[13]

Proper integration of knowledge into action takes practice. As implied in Aristotle's example of the beginning science student, we may be told and even concede that certain actions are good and noble without yet possessing a conviction that they have this intrinsic value. To adequately understand the intrinsic worth of these actions, more is needed than mere "head knowledge," assent to a proposition. The knowledge must be translated into "heart knowledge" as well.

---

[13]Risto Saarinen, *Weakness of the Will in Medieval Thought: From Augustine to Buridan* (New York: E. J. Brill, 1994), p. 15.

The student of right action must come to embrace in an affective way the actions that he has come to believe are right. And this takes time and practice, which is to say that this takes habituation.

The advance of this Aristotelian response to the problem of incontinence over that offered by Socrates comes from Aristotle's recognition that knowledge is often habit. For Socrates the power of knowledge resides in its content whereas for Aristotle the power of knowledge resides in the manner in which it is possessed by the knower. Whereas Socrates thinks that it should be enough for continent action that an agent merely possess knowledge, Aristotle recognizes that the knowledge must inform who we are, including our desires, if it is to be effective. Socrates says, "We must realize that each of us is ruled by two principles which we follow wherever they lead: one is our inborn desire for pleasures, the other is our acquired judgment that pursues what is best. Sometimes these two are in agreement; but there are times when they quarrel inside us, and then sometimes one of them gains control, sometimes the other."[14] But for Aristotle, there is a third principle—habit—that mediates between these two principles, incorporating them into each other. Whereas for Socrates we can never be sure which principle may gain control— "sometimes one of them gains control, sometimes the other"—Aristotle believes that we shape our lives just to the extent that our desires are informed by our knowledge and our knowledge is informed by our desires. Embodied knowledge, therefore, rather than "knowledge simple" or "abstract knowledge" is required for consistent continent and virtuous action, and incontinent action is often due to a lack of embodied knowledge—that is, to a failure of habit.

Whereas vehement or resilient passion is the source of impetuous incontinence, habit or the lack thereof is the source of what Aristotle calls "weak incontinence" and what commentators have more helpfully labeled "clear-eyed incontinence" since the agent acts contrary

---

[14]Plato, *Phaedrus*, trans. Alexander Nehamas and Paul Woodruff, in *Plato: Complete Works* (Indianapolis: Hackett, 1997), 237d-238a.

to what he can "see" to be true. The most perplexing forms of addictive behavior may be understood as instances of clear-eyed incontinence. Take the following recollection of a young female alcoholic.

> I picked up a half gallon of whisky one day after work and drank over one-third of it in less than four hours that same night. I was so sick the next day, but I made it to work. When I got home from work, I sat on my parents' sofa and knew, *I knew*, I would start working on the half gallon again, despite the fact that I was still very ill from the night before. I also knew that I did not want to drink. Sitting on that sofa, I realized that the old "I could stop if I wanted to, I just don't want to" didn't apply here, because I did not want to drink. I watched myself get up off the sofa and pour myself a drink. When I sat back down on the sofa, I started to cry. My denial had cracked; I believe I hit bottom that night, but I didn't know it then; I just thought I was insane. I proceeded to finish the half gallon. (AA 324)

This is an extreme case of incontinence. Indeed, the way the addict describes her experience communicates an overwhelming sense of compulsion, and we can only know that she was not unqualifiedly compelled because she eventually stopped drinking in a nonmedicalized program of recovery. What is being described is an experience of clear-eyed incontinence. She *watches herself* pour another drink. She knows that she should not drink, but she also knows that she will. This is a powerful depiction of the "divided self," a phenomenon that is central to addictive experience. And yet this is precisely in line with the character of weak or clear-eyed incontinence. The agent is in definite possession of the knowledge that she should not drink, yet she drinks anyway. We are not dealing here with a case of craving interrupting the deliberative process. In fact, strong passion does not obviously enter into the picture here at all. She drinks against her own better judgment and even against what seems to be her predominant desire. She knows she should not drink; she does not want to drink; yet she drinks. How is this possible? The bafflement of this kind of case far exceeds that of any form of impetuous incontinence.

If, as I have suggested, there is a power other than passion that can give us insight into the nature of some especially perplexing kinds of incontinence, then surely accounts like this one demand an investigation of such a power. If we are to penetrate the more baffling components of addictive experience, we will need to examine the nature of habit. Incontinence in all of its varieties cannot be comprehended on the basis of the features of ignorance or passion alone. The relationship between habit and incontinence may be the source of many of the most perplexing aspects of addictive experience.

To sum up: I have used Aristotle's philosophy of human action as a tool for narrowing our discussion to focus on that which is most perplexing about addictive behavior. Addictive behavior is sometimes beyond the scope of human action (morbid addiction) and sometimes straightforward vice (indulgent addiction). However, insofar as most addictive behavior is recognized by the addicted person to be destructive, and insofar as most instances of addictive behavior are remediable through nonmedical recovery models, most addictive behavior falls within the category of incontinent action. Aristotle provides two sorts of explanation of incontinent action in general. The first explains incontinent action as a result of rashness, strong appetites or abnormal bodily states. This analysis can make sense of within-episode instances of addictive behavior, as well as instances of addictive behavior that can be traced to physical or psychological craving. However, this explanation leaves untouched those instances of addictive behavior that are most perplexing, namely addictive action that is undertaken by a sober and competent agent who is experiencing neither physical nor psychological craving. Such behavior is on display throughout the addictive process, but it is most pronounced in instances of relapse. In order to better understand this most puzzling feature of the addictive experience, we must turn to a more thorough examination of the claim that such instances of clear-eyed incontinence are to be analyzed in terms of the power of habit in human action.

3

ADDICTION AND HABIT

Resources in Aquinas

◆

The category of habit provides tools for analyzing human action in terms other than the standard binaries that characterize most contemporary theorizing about addiction. Indeed, many of the most mysterious features of addictive behavior become less perplexing if we think of addiction as an exercise of habit. For instance, interpreting addiction in light of the category of habit can illuminate why persons continue to act addictively even when they are rationally convinced they should not, why addicted persons speak of being compelled to act addictively yet are able to recover without medical intervention, and why addicted persons who have been in recovery for months or even years may suddenly relapse. In order to provide such analyses, we must examine more extensively the importance of habit in an account of human action. To do so, I turn to the thought of Thomas Aquinas, whose philosophy of action mirrors, and yet profoundly deepens, that of Aristotle.

According to Aquinas, the human will is a power that must be flexed in and through the process of deliberative action. It is not some measureless metaphysical faculty, not some third term separable from reason and appetite. The will, for Aquinas, is rational appetite, appetitive reason. Practical reasoning—that is, reasoning about how we should act—is like theoretical reasoning in that it demands effort, concentration and discipline. Just as we cannot do calculus indefinitely without exhausting ourselves, neither can we deliberate indefinitely about practical dilemmas without exhausting ourselves. Deliberative action is inherently fragile and unstable because it requires an agent with finite powers to engage in an activity that tends to deplete those powers.

Despite the privilege that both Aristotle and Aquinas grant to the human person in virtue of its unique rational nature, neither would suppose that the successful moral life is one of constant deliberative engagement. A life that is perpetually involved in dealing with moral crises of action will inevitably be a failure. The problem with such crises, for Aquinas, is not that they are irresolvable, but rather that they tax the moral agent. The goal of moral training is the formation of moral habits because habit names the possibility of acting well without the exertion that is required of deliberative practical reasoning.

Aquinas does not consider crises of the will failures. They are inevitable, even for those with right habits, because habits sometimes come into conflict. Deliberative "choice" is what must take place when habits collide. But since an agent is incapable of sustaining indefinitely the kind of vigilance required for right practical reasoning, such crises, although providing opportunity for creative action, will end in failure unless they quickly become integrated into patterns of habitual thought and behavior. Thus for Aquinas, thinking well about human action requires us to investigate what sorts of things habits are, whether there are different kinds of habits, and how habits are caused.

AQUINAS ON HABIT

Aquinas says that habits are not necessary for humans to act, but they are necessary for humans to act well. This claim comes in Question 49, Article 4 of the *Prima Secundae*, "Whether Habits are Necessary." The article is central to everything that Aquinas goes on to say about the role of habit in human action. In this article, Aquinas makes the ambitious claim that habit *(habitus)*[1] must be included as an irreducible component of any ontology that is adequate to the scope of human action. His claim of the irreducibility of the category of habit is ambitious because, at first glance, it looks like we could explain every human action by referring it to the power of human will alone. Taking any one human action, we seem to be able to explain that action solely by referring to the power of human will. Habit therefore becomes superfluous as a principle of explanation, and if so, not a necessary component of an ontology of human action.[2]

Aquinas responds to this objection with two claims, but before doing so he states the nature of a habit and what kinds of things might have them. Namely, Aquinas argues that since habits involve dispositions to act in one way out of a variety of potential ways, the only things which have habits are rational actors whose natures do not entail their behavior. So there is "no room for habit" in God because God's action is identical to God's being. And there is no room for habit in nonrational things (including nonrational animals) because nonrational things are always determined by nature (in the case of animals, by "instinct") to respond in one way to any given situation. If we could know everything about an animal's needs and the circumstances the animal is in, we could know how the animal will respond. The animal, therefore, is never at one time actually open to more than one course of action. Thus habits belong to rational

---

[1]How to translate *habitus* is a perennial question among Aquinas scholars. In the introduction to *St. Thomas Aquinas: Summa Theologiae*, vol. 22, *Dispositions for Human Acts*, trans. Anthony Kenny (London: Blackfriars, 1964), Anthony Kenny argues that it should be translated as "disposition" rather than "habit." For reasons that will become clear, this seems to me to be an unhelpful and misguided translation. I will, therefore, despite all of the possible confusion that might result from the contemporary use of the word *habit*, continue to use "habit" for Aquinas's *habitus*.

[2]This seems to be the assumption guiding contemporary analytic philosophy of action. I have found only one essay on the theme of habit in what would be considered contemporary "action theory": Timothy Duggan's "Habit," in *Time and Cause: Essays Presented to Richard Taylor*, ed. Peter van Inwagen (London: D. Riedel, 1980). As an exercise in analytic philosophy, however, this article is limited to how people use the word *habit* today. It is therefore an example of the attenuated conception of habit that Aristotle and Aquinas help us move beyond.

animals only, namely to human beings,[3] whose existence is not identical with their activity and who may be capable of various alternative courses of action.

Habit, we are told, *could* make sense as an explanation of why a particular human agent acts one way or another, since we cannot explain the action simply with reference to the agent's essence (as with God) or simply with reference to some determined causal connection between the agent's needs and her environment (as with animals). But then again, the power of will could just as well be offered as an explanation, so Aquinas's ambitious thesis that habit is *necessary* to a full account of human action has not yet been vindicated. Aquinas provides two arguments to defend his thesis.

First, we must posit the category of habit to explain how it is possible that human beings can *tend* toward one among a variety of potential actions. Postulation of human will explains why it is *possible* in a given situation that an agent act in any of several ways. But it cannot explain what is also true—that it is sometimes *probable* that an agent will act one way rather than another.

Second, and relatedly, what stands in need of explanation is not merely each single event taken separately in an agent's history of action but also an agent's ability to act consistently over a prolonged period of time. This requires explanation because the human will is not (as Descartes supposed) an inexhaustible, abstract power, but rather an embodied power. Human will is executed through the material conditions of human personhood. As Aquinas puts it, although will is a function of the soul, the operations of the will proceed "from the soul through the body" (1-2.50.1). We cannot, therefore, pretend that the will is unconstrained by the body. This is why Aquinas says that habits of the will, although primarily habits of the soul, are secondarily habits of the body (1-2.50.1). Like the intellect and the sense appetite, practical reason—the "rational appetite"—is subject

---

[3]Aquinas thinks there is room for habits in angels too (1-2.50.6).

to alteration, corruption and exhaustion. Deliberative choice is carried out, not by transcending the desires naturally conditioned by our material existence, but through the exertion of the intellect, by ordering those desires. The will has a structure, susceptible to being trained but also therefore susceptible to breaking down. Given this fact, the consistent exercise of the will in any one direction is in need of explanation. A principle of explanation beyond the mere power of human will is needed to account for how the will perseveres in courses of action that would exhaust the will were it operating purely through deliberation. In the absence of habit, the will is subjected to the violence of competing impulses, and it cannot bear up consistently under such internal violence.

Habit supplies the needed principle of explanation. Habit explains how the will can act consistently and successfully without being worn down by the weight of desire or tripped up by uncoordinated desires because habits qualify and coordinate desires. Many habits, and in particular many of the virtues, cannot be understood apart from the passions to which they give shape and coordination. For Aquinas, habits are fundamentally strategies of desire.[4] I will be arguing in the next several chapters that this insight is central to rightly describing the power of addiction since addictions are among the most powerful strategies that human persons have for coordinating and directing their most fundamental desires.

Specifically, habits strategically rectify the problem of limited human will in two ways. First, habits are difficult to change: "We call habits those qualities which, by reason of their very nature, are not easily changed" (1-2.49.2). That habits should be difficult to change is a necessary correlate to their function, which is to provide stability and consistency to human action. Human action as exercised through the process of practical reasoning is inherently tenuous precisely because that on which the process is thoroughly depen-

---

[4] I owe this way of putting it to Paul J. Wadell, C.P., *The Primacy of Love: An Introduction to the Ethics of Thomas Aquinas* (New York: Paulist Press, 1992).

dent, namely passions and judgments, can be easily lost, ignored or overcome. Incontinent action, we have seen, is possible for this very reason. Therefore, if habits are to provide a kind of constancy not available through unrooted practical reasoning, they must be the sorts of things difficult to change or lose. If our habits can be changed as easily as our minds or our feelings, they provide no alternative to the shaky character of deliberative reasoning. The more entrenched the habit, the more perfectly it performs its task. Thus habits are qualities that (a) make an agent consistent in his or her actions; (b) make an agent successful in his or her action; and (c) make the "thing be done with ease" (1-2.49.2). These characteristics of habit are tightly interconnected. It is the stable permanence of habit that makes habitual action consistent. This consistency is possible because the action does not tax the agent's will in the way that deliberative action does. Thus the ease with which the agent acts habitually is, in addition to being a source of pleasure (1-2.53.1), that which secures the consistency of habitual action.

Second, habits rectify the problem of limited human will by their propensity to act "on cue." Aquinas says that since pleasure can be anticipated through the faculty of memory, a person may become disposed in such a way as to react habitually to the slightest provocation of that memory (1-2.33.2). When presented with the appropriate object, a habituated agent is able to act at once, without effort and often without any explicit consciousness of what is being done. Nevertheless, although habits do not require an act of deliberative will to be provoked, they are open to being interrupted by a specific act of the will. In this respect, they are importantly distinct from instincts.

We can now provide a robust definition of "habit." A habit is a relatively permanent acquired modification of a person that enables the person, when provoked by the relevant stimulus, to act consistently, successfully and with ease with respect to some objective.[5]

---

[5]Throughout the development of this definition, I have been dependent on George Klubertanz, *Habits and Virtues: A Philosophical Analysis* (New York: Appleton-Century-Crofts, 1965); and

HABIT AS A MEDIATING CATEGORY

The debate being waged within the field of addiction studies is couched in the language of disease versus choice. Now that we have defined the notion of habit, we can begin to explore how the category of habit makes room for a description of addictive behavior that avoids the binaries on offer in the current debate. Habit is a mediating category, but carefully articulating the nature of this mediation is an important step because, if we do not see how habit occupies a genuinely unique space within an ontology of human action, we are likely to collapse even the language of habit right back into the polarizing extremes that we are trying to escape. This is indeed what has happened to the language of habit in the contemporary debate in addiction studies. Because the category of habit is poorly understood, it has been blithely dismissed as an unhelpful or even pernicious way of characterizing addictive behavior.

Habit, properly understood, mediates between several different extremes that bound our conception of human action. First, habit mediates between instinct and disposition. Second, habit mediates between determinism and voluntarism. Third, habit mediates between the involuntary and the voluntary.

First, a habit is neither an instinct nor a disposition,[6] but it mediates between the two. A habit is like an instinct in that it can make action easy and seemingly effortless. Sometimes a habit can make it possible for an agent to act without conscious thought, and this is why habits are easily confused with instincts. Thus, for example, Brian Davies is confused when he writes that Aquinas "is concerned with the acquiring of character which enables people to act instinctively."[7] Aquinas could not have considered this an achieve-

---

Robert Brennan, *Thomistic Psychology: A Philosophic Analysis of the Nature of Man* (New York: Macmillan, 1941).

[6] For Aquinas, *habitus* belongs to the genus of *dispositio*, but can be distinguished from *dispositio* at the specific level (1-2.49.2). In this, Aquinas follows Aristotle: "Habits are at the same time dispositions, but dispositions are not necessarily habits," *Categories* 9a10-11, trans. E. M. Edghill, in *The Basic Works of Aristotle*, ed. Richard McKeon (New York: Random House, 1941).

[7] Brian Davies, *Introduction to* De Malo *by Thomas Aquinas,* trans. Richard Regan (Oxford: Oxford University Press, 2003), p. 31.

ment, since instinct names a tendency toward action that is not in any way responsive to reason. Davies's mistake comes from a penchant, present in early twentieth-century psychology, to take motor habits as the paradigm for all habits. If we think of all habits as being patterned on motor habits, we see how easily habits can be mistaken for instinct, since motor habits are most effective to the extent that we do not mentally focus on how to do the activities they make possible. As William James pointed out, you will be much more efficient at tying your shoes if you refrain from thinking about how to do it.

But Aquinas would insist that even motor habits, which have salient characteristics similar to those of instinct, are different from instincts in that they can be blocked and transformed, usually over much time and with great effort, by the application of reason. Instincts are not like this. Instinct can be transformed only by operant conditioning, as is the case with animals: "The sensitive powers of dumb animals do not act at the command of reason; but if they are left to themselves, such animals act from natural instinct: and so in them there are no habits ordained to operations" (1-2.50.3). An instinct does not imply the power to refrain from the instinctual action, whereas a habit does imply this power. Animals "have not that power of using or of refraining, which seems to belong to the notion of habit: and therefore, properly speaking, there can be no habits in them" (1-2.50.3). We must therefore be careful to maintain a distinction between instinct and habit, lest by obscuring the distinction we obscure one of the most important characteristics of habit: its responsiveness to reason and, therefore, its connection with the voluntary.

But we must also note the similarities between habit and instinct, and this will enable us to see how Davies and others might confuse the two. For when we say that habit, unlike instinct, is responsive to reason, that should not be taken to imply that habitual actions can be arrested and habits dispelled (or, on the other hand, habitual actions incited and habits acquired) simply by performing an act of will. On the contrary, habits, like instincts, take on a life of their own and often provoke "on cue" actions that are quite recalcitrant to whatever momentary intention an agent might possess. This is why Aristotle says that "habit is hard to change because it is like nature" (1152a30-31), and why Aquinas, following Aristotle, tells us that "a habit is like a second nature" (1-2.53.1).[8] Indeed, it is precisely the similarity of addictive action to the true compulsions of instinct that has led (given the contemporary loss of a robust philosophy of habit) to the assimilation of addiction to the purely involuntary category of disease. Despite their similarities, however, Aquinas insists that habits are different from instincts because habits are responsive to reason. But when Aquinas says that habits, unlike instinct, are responsive to reason, he is not thinking primarily in terms of the power of rational deliberation to overcome habitual actions "on the spot," although this is at times possible. Rather, Aquinas is interested in the way in which reason can develop strategies, manipulate circumstances and inform alternative modes of character. In this way, reason can gradually and indirectly transform habits and the corresponding actions that they elicit.

Conversely, there is a danger of confusing a habit with a disposition. A habit is like a disposition in that it can be changed. But a habit is unlike a disposition in that it cannot be changed without great effort. Dispositions are different from habits "in the point of being easily or difficultly lost," respectively: "The word *habit* implies a certain lastingness; the word *disposition* does not" (1-2.49.2). Thus, for example, Aquinas would think that being generous and speaking French are habits, whereas biting one's nails or saying "Dude!" a lot are probably dispositions. The distinction between habitual and dispositional behaviors rests on the difficulty encoun-

---

[8]In his *Commentary on Aristotle's* Nicomachean Ethics, trans. C. I. Litzinger, O.P. (Notre Dame, Ind.: Dumb Ox Books, 1993), #1370, Aquinas suggests that a habit, for Aristotle, "brings about a quasi-nature."

tered when a person tries to quit the behavior. If the behavior is deeply entrenched and requires much effort, creativity and ingenuity to quit, then the behavior counts as a habit for Aquinas. If the behavior is not (yet) deeply entrenched and can be rooted out simply by recognizing that it is problematic, it is likely not a habit but a mere disposition. Often a tendency is more or less entrenched depending on the degree to which the tendency implicates an agent's emotions. Thus, frequently picking one's nose is more often than not a dispositional tendency, whereas frequently smoking is more often than not a habitual tendency.

The distinction between habit and disposition is plagued by a certain vagueness. By what standards are we to decide whether a particular tendency to act has or has not enough "lastingness" to be considered a habit? No set of standards can decisively remove this ambiguity; there will always be borderline cases. But this should not lead us to discount the importance of the distinction. The distinction between habit and disposition is not, for Aquinas, merely arbitrary: "These differences, though apparently accidental to quality, nevertheless designate differences which are proper and essential to quality" (1-2.49.2).

Careful attention to how habit mediates between instinct and disposition enables us to avoid twin dangers that stalk the language of habit in the contemporary discussion of addiction. One such tendency is to conflate habit and instinct, thereby dismissing the claim that addiction is a habit. This sort of mistake is evident in the following passage from Francis Seeburger:

> In the final analysis, there is nothing "habitual" about injecting oneself with narcotics twice a day over a prolonged period. Something that has become habitual is something one has learned to do without thinking about it. That is the role of habit: to allow us to do things without having to bother to think about doing them, or about what we are doing while we do them. Thus, for example, after we struggle long enough with them, the movements and bodily adjustments in-

volved in riding a bicycle or in swimming become habitual to us, so that when we climb on a bike or jump into a swimming pool we don't have to think about what we are supposed to do; we just do it. That description does not, however, fit the case of someone injecting himself or herself with heroin twice a day. On the contrary . . . addicts quite consciously invest the whole activity of their drug taking with significance. They tend to ritualize it, sometimes giving even the most trivial surrounding circumstances the status of inviolable rites.[9]

As is apparent from the examples Seeburger gives, he assumes that motor habits are paradigmatic habits, and, therefore, that a lack of thought pertaining to the action under question is a necessary property of habit. Habit has been conflated with instinct, as an unthinking response in a particular situation. But for Aquinas, this would be an odd restriction on habit, not least because Aquinas believes that one of the faculties of persons that can become habituated is the intellect. In describing the ritual tendencies of addictive behavior, Seeburger has pinpointed the crucial meaning-making function of addiction (and thus a crucial connection between addiction and rationality). He has not, however, given us any reason to think that addictive behavior is nonhabitual.

Conversely, habit may be wrongly conflated with disposition, thereby dismissing the prospect that addiction is a habit. So, for example, one reads in the literature of A.A. that certain types of alcoholics discovered that they did not "just" have a bad habit of drinking alcohol, but that, indeed, they were alcoholics: "By going back in our own drinking histories, we could show that years before we realized it we were out of control, that our drinking even then was *no mere habit*, that it was indeed the beginning of a fatal progression"

---

[9]Francis Seeburger, *Addiction and Responsibility: An Inquiry into the Addictive Mind* (New York: Crossroad, 1993), pp. 45-46. It is worth noting, however, that despite this explicit rejection of thinking of addiction in terms of habit, Seeburger, in part because he is careful to avoid the categories of disease and compulsion, cannot help slipping back into thinking of addiction in terms of habit: "The best way to define the alcoholic is not as someone who habitually *drinks*, but as someone who habitually *chooses* to drink" (p. 90). I am not sure this is the best way to define the alcoholic, but Seeburger is right that alcoholism has something to do with habit.

(TT 23, emphasis mine). The adjective "mere" is telling here. If one reads this passage further, it becomes clear that a distinction is being sought between those who may be "merely" problem-drinkers and those who are "full-blooded" alcoholics. But what distinguishes a problem-drinker from an alcoholic is precisely what distinguishes, for Aquinas, a disposition from a habit. A problem-drinker has a tendency to drink, but upon recognizing the ill effects of her behavior she is able to stop drinking more or less straightforwardly, without drastic measures. The alcoholic, on the other hand, may recognize the nature of her problem without being able to root out the tendency to drink simply by deciding to do so. Both problem-drinkers and alcoholics have tendencies toward alcohol, but one tendency is easily lost and the other is not. This parallels exactly the distinction that Aquinas wishes to make between a disposition and a habit. Aquinas would say that an alcoholic has a habit, though by no means a *mere* habit (this would be oxymoronic for Aquinas) of drinking, whereas a problem-drinker has a disposition to drink. Habit language has been wrongly dismissed from reflection on addiction because it has been incorrectly conflated with either instinct or disposition. But in fact habit occupies a genuine space between the two.

Second, the category of habit mediates between the extremes of determinism and voluntarism. Habitual action is like autonomous free will in that it connects up at some level with reason. On the other hand, habitual action is like determinism in that the actions performed by habit do not issue directly from the process of deliberative reasoning that is constitutive of free will. We have already noticed Aquinas's notion of a habit as a "second nature": "A habit is like a second nature, and yet it falls short of it. And so it is that while the nature of a thing cannot in any way be taken away from a thing, a habit is removed, though with difficulty" (1-2.53.2). If something acts a certain way "by nature," that thing is determined to so act. In animals, we call that instinct. A habit is a "second nature" because, although it is not strictly speaking mechanical, it nevertheless proceeds from the agent effortlessly and without exertion of will, apparently "naturally." Mariana Valverde nicely summarizes the way in which habit mediates between determinism and free will. Habits are "patterned acts that are neither fully willed nor completely automatic," which "inhabit the hybrid zone, often known as second nature, that has always been neglected by theology and philosophy."[10]

Valverde's comment about the neglect of the category of habit among theologians and philosophers is interesting given the aims of this study. Such neglect has not always been the case. As Valverde rightly notes, "in Aristotle's time theorizing habit was the fundamental business of professional ethical philosophers."[11] Valverde overlooks the medieval tradition, including Aquinas, but she rightly points out the relative absence of a philosophy of habit through the modern period, with the notable exceptions of the American pragmatists, particularly William James, Charles Peirce and John Dewey.[12] Habit was reintroduced into the discussions of early twentieth-century psychology and the philosophy of human action as a corrective to exaggerated claims about the scope of absolute freedom of volition. James, for example, speaks of the "force of habit" precisely to show that most human action is not nearly so "free" as certain philosophies of a vaunted free will would lead us to suppose. But, strangely, the role of habit-language in the contemporary discourse on addiction has undergone a reversal. No longer is habit introduced as a corrective to an overemphasis on freedom and volition but rather, in the opposite direction, habit is rejected by the

---

[10]Mariana Valverde, *Diseases of the Will: Alcohol and the Dilemmas of Freedom* (Cambridge: Cambridge University Press, 1998), pp. 36-37.

[11]Ibid., p. 40.

[12]Although William James's work on habit was immensely important for the renascence of the concept of habit in early twentieth-century psychology, little in his work on habit had not been covered more thoroughly by Aristotle and Aquinas. Furthermore, I worry that James focuses too narrowly on motor habits as the paradigm in terms of which other habits are to be explained. This criticism does not apply to John Dewey's *Human Nature and Conduct*, ed. Jo Ann Boydston (Carbondale: Southern Illinois University Press, 1983). Although Dewey is not a primary interlocutor for me, his is the best modern treatment of the category of habit that I know.

proponents of the disease concept as a veiled attempt to smuggle choice back into the equation. What is important to see in all of this is that habit genuinely stands midway between *both* determined disease *and* unconstrained choice, and therefore acts as an important corrective in both directions. To say "addiction is a habit" is to say something genuinely different from either "addiction is a disease" or "addiction is a choice" because habit mediates between determinism and voluntarism.

Third and finally, habit mediates between the voluntary and the involuntary. For, as we have already mentioned, habits qualify desires. Craig Steven Titus puts the point succinctly: Aquinas shows us how habits "instill intelligence in emotions."[13] But if this is so, then we cannot easily make the customary distinction between actions as things that we make happen and emotions as things that happen to us, between actions as purely voluntary and emotions as purely involuntary. Habit names the possibility of partial responsibility for and control over our emotions. For both Aristotle and Aquinas, it is within our power, for example, to develop the habit of courage, which is to say that it is within our power both to develop our tendency to *act* in a certain way in circumstances that call for courage and to develop our tendency to *feel* a certain way in those circumstances.

Thus the category of habit complicates our everyday view of the voluntary/involuntary distinction. In his *Commentary on Aristotle's "Nicomachean Ethics,"* Aquinas explains how habits simultaneously bear characteristics of the voluntary and of the involuntary.

> Evil habits are not subject to the will after they have been formed. He says that because a person becomes unjust voluntarily, it does not fol-

---

.[13]Craig Steven Titus, *Resilience and the Virtue of Fortitude: Aquinas in Dialogue with the Psychosocial Sciences* (Washington, D.C.: Catholic University of America Press, 2006), p. 116. A fascinating neurological confirmation of this comes from Christiane Northrup, M.D., who says, "Not only do our physical organs contain receptor sites for the neurochemicals of thought and emotion, our organs and immune systems *can themselves manufacture these same chemicals.* What this means is that our entire body feels and expresses emotion—all parts of us 'think' and 'feel.' . . . *The mind is located throughout the body,*" quoted in Bruce Wilshire, *Wild Hunger: The Primal Roots of Modern Addiction* (Lanham, Md.: Rowman and Littlefield, 1998), p. 74.

low that he ceases to be unjust and becomes just whenever he may will. He proves this by means of a likeness in the dispositions of the body. A man who in good health willingly falls into sickness by living incontinently, i.e., by eating and drinking to excess and not following the doctor's advice, had it in his power in the beginning not to become sick. But after he has performed the act, having eaten unnecessary or harmful food, it is no longer in his power not to be sick. Thus he who throws a stone is able not to throw it; however once he has thrown the stone he has not the power to take back the throwing. Nevertheless we do say that it is within a man's power to cast or throw a stone because it was from a principle under his control. So it is also with the habits of vice; that a man not become unjust or incontinent arises from a principle under his control. Hence we say that men are voluntarily unjust and incontinent, although, after they have become such, it is no longer within their power to cease being unjust or incontinent immediately, but great effort and practice are required.[14]

To expand on Aquinas's insight: We might mean one of two things by calling something more or less voluntary. On the one hand, we might think of the ultimate in voluntarity as being that which is most expressive of an agent's character. Or, on the other hand, we might think of the ultimate in voluntarity as being that which is most susceptible to an agent's immediate control, in other words, as being that which an agent is most arbitrarily free to do or leave undone. If we take voluntarity in the first sense, habitual actions are indeed the most voluntary of our actions because they spring, not just from some fleeting deliberative process, but rather from the source of who we are, our character. If we take voluntarity in the second sense, habitual actions are indeed the least voluntary of our actions because, since they flow from deeply engrained habits, they are least susceptible to fleeting deliberations or desires to "do otherwise."

By mediating between the voluntary and the involuntary, habit

---

[14]Aquinas, *Commentary on Aristotle's "Nicomachean Ethics,"* #513.

confounds our common sense views about the realm of voluntary action. We customarily assume that the sphere of the voluntary is coterminous with the sphere of the autonomously willed. Put differently, we customarily assume a proportional relationship between responsibility and "the ability to do otherwise": the greater the arbitrary freedom to do otherwise, the greater our responsibility for our action. But for Aristotle and Aquinas, an inverse relationship exists between the two. Rather than implying that the problem is in some sense "external," the loss of immediate control over our actions may tell us that the problem is deeply "internal"; the problem may be in a sense one of *who we are*. This is not to say that addiction, rather than being a disease, is a symptom of especial moral depravity. I will in fact argue directly *against* this all-too-common view. But I will contend that rather than being things that we *have* (as diseases are), addictions are more like things that we *become*.

KINDS AND CAUSES OF HABIT

The aim of the preceding inquiry into the mediating character of habit was to create space between such binaries as instinct/disposition, determinism/voluntarism, voluntary/involuntary, and disease/choice—space that can be made intelligible as a locus of habit. But now we must ask more specifically about the kinds of habit that can occupy this space. Habits, we have seen, belong peculiarly to rational animals, namely human persons. But for Aquinas, habits belong to persons as qualifications of the powers (or faculties) of human persons. Therefore, we have to ask about these powers separately, whether and how they are susceptible to becoming habituated.

Aquinas undertakes this inquiry in Question 50 of the *Prima Secundae*, "Of the Subject of Habits." There he responds to questions about whether or not habits may be developed in the human body, the soul and, more particularly, the sensitive part of the soul, the intellectual part of the soul and the will. He answers yes to all these questions, although the body is said to be the subject of habits only analogously and imperfectly. We could, following Aquinas, ask about the capacity for habituation of each separate power of a human person, but this would take us too far from the center of our inquiry. So we shall have to ask about a select number of these powers, mainly those that will be shown to have direct bearing on the hypothesis that addiction is a rationally informed habit.

Broadly speaking, Aquinas analyzes the human person in terms of three "souls," each of which consists of a variety of powers: the vegetative, sensitive and intellectual souls. I am interested in the capacity for habituation of several of the subpowers of the sensitive soul. Among the powers of the sensitive soul are the interior powers of the imagination, the "evaluating sense" *(sensus aestimativus)* and the memory. Imagination is the power that allows for "the retention and preservation of [sensible] forms" (1.78.4). We do seem capable of developing certain habits of imagination. The skilled artist has developed a particular way of "seeing" the world and retaining that vision in her imagination. Artists do not have a modified external power of sight—they may be as far- or nearsighted as the next person—but artists have developed their imaginations in such a way that they "see" a world that differs from the one the non-artist sees. Or, similarly, someone who has been raised reading good fantasy literature might genuinely be equipped with more elaborate and creative imaginative skills than someone whose imagination has not been shaped in this way. This is what we mean when we speak of someone with an "impoverished imagination"; it is not that they lack the power of imagination, but that their power of imagination has not been habituated in the sorts of skills that belong to someone with a "rich imagination."

The *sensus aestimativus*, the "evaluating sense," enables a function similar to that of the imagination. Whereas the imagination allows for the apprehension of sensible things, the *sensus aestimativus* allows for "the apprehension of intentions which are not received through the senses" (1.78.4). By "intentions," Aquinas means the insensate qualities of objects, such as a thing's goodness or badness, suitability or unsuitability. Aquinas helps us grasp the function of the *sensus aestimativus* by first showing how the *sensus aestimativus* must function in animals. Nothing in a lamb's *sense perception* of a wolf warns the lamb that the wolf is bad, an enemy to be avoided. This information must come from elsewhere, and Aquinas says that it comes from the *sensus aestimativus* by which animals "perceive these intentions only by some natural instinct" (1.78.4).

Human persons have instincts too. Babies, for example, instinctively cry when a loud bang is made in front of their faces. In cases of extreme panic, human beings may act automatically and instinctively from fear. But our instincts are rudimentary as compared with those of other animals. Most of our immediate evaluations of the objects and situations we encounter are learned rather than instinctive. As Aquinas puts it, whereas animals perceive good and evil in objects by way of instinct, "man perceives them by means of coalition of ideas. Therefore the power which in other animals is called the natural estimative, in man is called the *cogitative*, which by some sort of collation discovers these intentions" (1.78.4). The cogitative estimative power, therefore, is the site of a "compenetration of reason into sense";[15] it is the paradigmatic locus of habit as *embodied knowledge*.

The important difference between the cogitative estimative power and the powers that belong to the intellectual soul—deliberative reason and will—is the immediacy with which the estimative power recognizes objects or situations as good or evil, suitable or unsuitable. The evaluation seems to *come with* the sensory experience, although it is of course impossible to perceive good or evil with the exterior senses. Whenever an immediate and definite link exists between a subject's perception of an object and the subject's appetency for the object, it is this link that the estimative power explains. In animals, the link comes already forged, a natural instinct. In human

---

[15]Klubertanz, *Habits and Virtues*, p. 46.

beings, however, the link is forged through reason, although not necessarily at the level of rational deliberation.

Because the cogitative estimation rarely acts in the absence of other powers, including deliberative rational judgment, it can be difficult to isolate. The most obvious examples are cases in which, in our contemporary idiom, we might say we just have an "intuition" that something is bad or inappropriate or unsuitable or, on the other hand, good, appropriate or suitable. For instance, when a person at a dinner party lacks tact, we *sense* this immediately, without any need for discursive analysis.[16] Indeed, we often might find it difficult to articulate why we consider this person to be tactless; we just know it when we *see* it. This kind of evaluation is obviously not a consequence of some explicit discursive process, but neither is it instinct. It is made possible by a long history of learning: learning manners from our elders, watching the reactions of persons we trust in social situations, feeling the displeasure of others when we make a social blunder and so on. This is why the estimation is *cogitative:* it is the effect of a "coalition of ideas," a reserve of learned wisdom that has become interwoven with the objects of our experience. It is not the effect of conditioning, which takes place in the absence of any appeal to reason, yet it operates immediately and without intellectual effort, as if by conditioning. Often, it is the reactions that issue from our cogitative estimations that get mistaken for "instinct."

The habituation of the cogitative estimation is the single most powerful component of addiction and the addictive experience. Although the language of "cogitative estimation" is not familiar to us, I will employ it frequently in the rest of the argument. In each case, we could describe things differently by speaking, for example, of the ways in which addiction recommends itself to an agent through appeal to an agent's "tacit knowing"—to use Michael Polanyi's description—rather than to an agent's "propositional reasoning."[17] The dis-

---

[16]The illustration comes from Klubertanz, *Habits and Virtues*, p. 34.

[17]On the notion of "tacit knowledge," see Michael Polanyi, *The Tacit Dimension* (Garden City,

tinction can be highlighted in numerous ways, some of them more intuitive and familiar to us than the distinction in Aquinas's faculty psychology between the intellect proper and the cogitative estimation. But I have preferred to refer back to the cogitative estimation in order to reiterate that, whatever the proper denotation of the source of this knowledge, that source is deeply susceptible to habituation. We are tempted to think that the source of our "tacit knowing" is in some sense primordial or unconditioned, but this is not so.

We move finally to the power of memory, which works in conjunction with the imagination and the cogitative estimation to enable the re-presentation of sensible forms and intentions. Were it not for the memorative power, the imagination and the cogitative estimation would be of little worth since it is through the memorative power that past accomplishments of the imagination and cogitative estimation are brought to bear on present action. But the habituation of memory is essentially derivative of the habituations of imagination and cogitative estimation. Because a person comes to "see" his or her world a certain way, his or her memory records the world a certain way and represents it to the agent as informed by the agent's habituated imagination.

Before moving forward in the investigation, I want to summarize one more general point about habit, namely how habits are caused and how they increase and decrease. Aquinas treats these matters in Questions 51 and 52 of the *Prima Secundae*. In Question 51, we are told that habits are formed by acts. In rare cases, one act is sufficient to form a habit. This is true, we are told, "if the active principle is of great power" (1-2.51.3). It does seem possible that one drink of alcohol or one hit of heroin, for instance, may be a sufficiently powerful

N.Y.: Doubleday, 1967). Although Polanyi broke new ground by showing how tacit knowledge could not be kept separate from the more "objective" knowledges pursued in modern science, the insight that our rationality extends beyond the propositional or discursive reaches back at least to Aristotle. William James called it the "sentiment of rationality" and offered a classic analysis in "The Sentiment of Rationality," in *The Writings of William James*, ed. John J. McDermott (Chicago: University of Chicago Press, 1977).

active principle to instantiate a habit. However, cases such as this are probably rarer than we are sometimes led to believe. The Big Book of A.A. states that "though there is no way of proving it, we believe that early in our drinking careers most of us could have stopped drinking. But the difficulty is that few alcoholics have enough desire to stop while there is yet time" (AA 32).

Most habits are caused by the repetition of acts which are proper to the habit. For instance, the habit of temperance is produced when a person who is not yet temperate nevertheless performs actions similar to those that would be performed by a temperate person. We cannot say that the would-be temperate person must perform the *same* actions as would be performed by a temperate person; this is impossible since the would-be temperate person does not yet possess the desires that make the temperate person's actions what they are. Nevertheless, if acts that are similar in outward form to those of the temperate person's "be multiplied[,] a certain quality is formed in the power which is passive and moved, which quality is called a habit" (1-2.51.2). If someone wants to become a skilled basketball player, she must repeatedly do as skilled basketball players do, even though, since she is not skilled, she will not be able to perform the actions with the same success, consistency and ease that a skilled player does. Over time, however, the repetition of such acts instills habits in the agent, permitting her to play basketball with skillful ease.

Repetition alone, however, is not sufficient to produce habits. In addition to the outward multiplication of like acts, an inward "intensity" of intent and focus is required. Alongside the repetition of external acts, we must also attend to the interior quality of acts. This is because a habit does not merely include the ability to perform external actions but also entails some sort of continuity between an agent's actions and her intentions and desires. Without attention to the interior quality of acts, we can at best become conditioned, but not habituated. The formation and growth of habits depends on this interior "intensity" of intent and desire: "So, too, repeated acts cause a habit to grow. If, however, the act falls short of the intensity of the habit, such an act does not dispose to an increase of that habit, but rather to a lessening thereof" (1-2.52.3). Habituation, therefore, occurs through external and internal exertion: "The same acts need to be repeated many times for anything to be firmly impressed on the memory," but also, "meditation strengthens memory" (1.51.3).

Aquinas's account of how habits are gained and lost provides an insight needed to begin sketching a theory of relapse. Relapse is the most distinctive and the most vexing aspect of the addictive experience. How can it be that, after days, weeks, months or even years of sobriety, a former addict can suddenly resume addictive behavior?

Aquinas says that habits are formed whenever two conditions are met. First, the external act must be repeated. Second, there must be appropriate attention to the interior quality of the acts. The life of recovery requires the development of new habits, but an addicted person may engage in the external acts necessary to the development of such habits without also undertaking the "internal" work necessary to the development of such habits. Thus an addicted person may fail to develop genuine habits of sobriety even as she appears outwardly to be "working the steps." Because the repetition of external acts is not sufficient for the growth of habits, the habits necessary for the life of recovery can be lacking or degenerating all the while an agent carries on like a person in recovery. As Robert Brennan states, "In the matter of habit, as in the matter of perfection, if we are not progressing, we are deteriorating."[18] Thus the A.A. adage: "If you're coasting in recovery, you're going downhill."[19] This is why many of the "steps" of A.A. call for inward or "spiritual" work.[20] "It is easy to

---

[18]Brennan, *Thomistic Psychology*, p. 269.

[19]William Cope Moyers with Katherine Ketcham, *Broken: My Story of Addiction and Redemption* (New York: Viking, 2006), p. 205.

[20]In *Thirst: God and the Alcoholic Experience* (Louisville: Westminster John Knox Press, 2004), James Nelson notes that the Twelve Steps alternate between calls to inward acceptance and appropriation of certain truths and calls to outward action. "There is the repeated recognition that *willingness* must precede our actual decision (willing) to take the steps that will open us to the gift of sobriety," p. 201 n.41.

let up on the spiritual program of action and rest on our laurels. We are headed for trouble if we do, for alcohol is a subtle foe" (AA 85). Failure to doggedly work the "spiritual" steps is referred to as "two-stepping" and is seen to be the primary threat to authentic and lasting recovery. Because recovery as conceived by A.A. is a technology of habit reformation, it demands vigilant attention to both the external and internal dimensions of sober action. Relapse is possible, in part, because the life of recovery is a life of re-habituation rather than merely a life of repetition of acts of abstinence.

ADDICTION AS HABIT

The category of habit provides a way of thinking through the mysteries and contradictions that plague every discourse of addiction that is couched either in terms of disease or of willful choice. It turns out that human action is largely the domain of habit. Not only how we respond, but also the way in which we see the situations we confront and the alternatives open to us are thoroughly drenched in habit. Although the language is slightly overblown, we begin to see how John Dewey could claim, "Concrete habits are the means of knowledge and thought. . . . Concrete habits do all the perceiving, recognizing, imagining, recalling, judging, conceiving and reasoning that is done. 'Consciousness,' whether as a stream or as special sensations and images, expresses functions of habits, phenomena of their formation, operation, their interruption and reorganization."[21]

Human action is often the confluence point of passion and rational judgment. Impetuous incontinence is possible at this point because of the cunning of passion; passion puts itself under the nose of the deliberating agent, distracting the agent from connecting up the right universal judgment with the right particular judgment. But even in the absence of vehement or resilient passion, an agent is not secure from the threat of incontinence, for human action is also

---

[21]Dewey, *Human Nature and Conduct*, pp. 123-24.

the confluence point of rational judgment and habit. Indeed, before deliberation begins, habits of imagination, habits of cogitative estimation, habits of appetite and habits of intellect are already operative, constituting the means by which the agent discerns her situation, including the various available actions. Often, rational deliberation is only necessary when there is some conflict between these habits. Under normal circumstances, the habits of the agent enable the agent to act well or ill with ease, success and consistency. However, when there is a conflict between habits, the habits do not thereby vanish. Rather, they vie for precedence as the agent struggles to navigate her situation.

Because it is presented by Aristotle and Aquinas as the territory between the habits of vice and virtue, it is natural to envision the territory of continence and incontinence as a sort of habit-free zone in which the primary contenders are pure reason and brute appetites. However, this is not so. The territory of continence and incontinence is rather the territory in which habits collide, negotiating and adjudicating their own increase and decrease, their making and unmaking. Since habits are the embodiment of knowledge—reserve "pockets of thought"[22] that fund human activity—the territory of incontinence is therefore the territory in which knowledges collide: the abstract knowledges of deliberation confront the embodied knowledges of habit. This is why incontinence is possible in the absence of vehement or resilient passion.

The consistent failure of the addicted person even in the absence of vehement or resilient desire can be explained by the role that habits play in the formation and execution of moral agency. Incontinence often has to do with the cunning and power of passion, but

---

[22]M. F. Burnyeat, "Aristotle on Learning to Be Good," in *Essays on Aristotle's Ethics*, ed. Amelie O. Rorty (Berkeley: University of California Press, 1980), p. 80, describes certain habits as "pockets of thought which can remain relatively unaffected by our overall view of things." I do not think these "pockets" can remain unaffected if they really are in conflict with our *overall* view of things, but they certainly can remain unaffected by the ebb and flow of practical deliberation.

the qualitatively distinct incontinence of addiction is, although sometimes an effect of passion, characteristically the result of the sway of habit. The most baffling phenomena of the incontinence of addictive experience can be illuminated as we come to understand the ways in which embodied knowledges—certain kinds of habits—exercise far-reaching and colossal power over human action. In particular, habits of imagination and the cogitative estimation play a decisive role in cases of addictive incontinence that cannot be explained with reference to passion. For since right action depends at some point on the integration of deliberative knowledge into action, right action meets definite resistance wherever deliberation arrives at conclusions that conflict with knowledges already embodied as habits of imagination or cogitative estimation.

Thus in the most perplexing cases of addictive behavior, we are confronted, not with reason struggling against appetite or emotion, but rather with free-floating reason struggling against reason as rooted in habits of the imagination and the cogitative estimation. If addiction is habit, then we should expect addicted persons to describe their experiences in the language of compulsion and instinct yet nevertheless to find nonmedical means of ameliorating their behavior. If addiction is habit, then it is unsurprising that the addictive experience is described as qualitatively distinct from other "mere bad habits" (dispositions). If addiction is habit, then the frequent occurrence of relapse after days, weeks or even years of abstinence becomes less baffling. And if addiction resides in habits of the imagination and cogitative estimation, then it becomes less surprising that addicted persons continue to engage in addictive behavior even when they are rationally convinced that doing so is to their own detriment. Exposing the ways that reason becomes embedded in habits of thought and imagination permits us to articulate how these and other peculiarities of addictive behavior are possible.

4

ADDICTION
AND INTEMPERANCE

Sensory Pleasures and Moral Goods

◆

This chapter extends and deepens the analysis of addiction as habit by addressing two further questions. First, what type of habit is addiction? Second, toward what sorts of ends or goals is the habit of addiction directed? The answers to these questions will challenge many of our clichéd moralistic caricatures of addicts and addictive behavior. According to popular belief, addiction is a rejection or abnegation of a life of serious moral endeavor, and addicted persons are therefore morally dubious individuals. In opposition to this standard view, I contend that addiction is in fact a deeply moral undertaking directed toward the attainment of particular moral and intellectual goods. Such an analysis will provide a more truthful assessment of the lure of addiction. It will also provoke a more compassionate response to addicted persons. Finally, such an analysis will put us in a position to recognize the ways in which all of us are both susceptible to addiction and implicated in ways of life that invite and foster addictions in ourselves and others.

COMPLEX HABITS

In the previous chapter, we investigated several powers of human agents taken singly in order to discover which of them was subject to habituation: the imagination, the memory and the *sensus aestimativus* or cogitative estimation. The investigation uncovered what may be called "simple habits," habits involving one habit and one power. In concrete human activity, however, powers rarely act in isolation from one another. Indeed, the fact that human powers do not ordinarily work separately but rather in cooperation with one another creates the main obstacle to isolating simple habits. The elucidation of simple habits, therefore, can only be preliminary to a fuller elaboration of the ways in which simple habits combine and cohere to form habit groups—"complex habits" which involve the cooperation of two or more habituated powers.

The virtue of temperance provides an example of the way in which intelligible human action most often involves the integration of a number of simple habits into a coordinated habit group. Temperance is properly a qualification of the sensory appetite; it has to do with having the right kinds of bodily desires. But although temperance substantially resides in the sensory appetite, it requires the ordered cooperation of several different powers. As a modification of the sensory appetite, temperance names the achievement of a consistent and appropriate mode of tendency toward sensible goods. Temperance, therefore, requires habituation of the passions. Temperance has to do not only with right *action* with respect to sensible goods, but also with right *desire* for sensible goods; it entails a proportionate or rightly measured reaction to such goods, both in terms of desire and act. But how is this proportionate response to be attained?

Temperance does not consist in eating a set amount of food each day, but rather in eating a suitable amount of food, taking into consideration the individual and his circumstances. As Aristotle reminds us, the temperate amount of food for the wrestler Milo will be excessive for the beginner in athletic exercises (1106b4-5). So the right habituation of the sense appetites requires the cooperation and habituation of other human powers, namely the habituation of intellect that makes possible the formal determination of the suitable amount of food for the agent. Furthermore, once the suitable measure is determined by the intellect, this measure cannot be simply imposed on the sensory appetite directly except by doing violence to the person's agency. The intellect cannot simply demand to the sense appetites "this is what you shall desire." The link between the intellect's determination of the suitable measure and the sensory appetite's right desire for that measure—the link which consists in the estimation of the suitable measure as good—must be established through habituation of the cogitative estimation. Temperance, therefore, requires the coordination of habits of sensory appetite, intellect and cogitative estimation. In Aquinas's technical terminology, the complex habit of temperance is substantially in the power of sensory appetite and formally in the intellectual power including the power of the cogitative estimation. We could continue the trajectory and show how habituation of the imagination and memory must also be integrated into the habit group of temperance.

Aquinas claims that habits are necessary because "in disposing the subject to one of those things to which it is in potentiality, several things should occur, capable of being adjusted in various ways: so as to dispose the subject well or ill to its form or to its operation" (1-2.49.4). Having noted the complexity of the habit group required to make temperate action consistent and successful, we are in a position to appreciate the force of this observation. The person who wishes to act temperately but lacks any of the numerous simple habits that coordinate to form the habit group of temperance is like the would-be painter who has developed his skills of the palette without bothering to learn the basic laws of perspective that are required to "see" the world in such a way that it can be rendered vividly and effectively. Such a person is not an artist at all, but merely one who may reproduce the work of other artists. Similarly, one who does not possess all of the simple habits constitutive of temperance cannot be temperate but only, at best, continent, since temperance is a complex habit that requires the alignment of numerous faculties of the human person.

Most complex habits consist of at least two different types of habit: mastery habits and automatism habits.[1] Mastery habits are those habits that can be exercised only through the operation of rational consciousness or volition. Habits of intellect (prudence, theoretical science, understanding) and habits of will (justice) are the most obvious mastery habits. One cannot engage in the habitual practice of prudence without simultaneously engaging a habituated intellect. Automatism habits, on the other hand, can be exercised in the absence of rational consciousness. Habits of the imagination (including motor habits) and cogitative estimation are the most obvious candidates for the category of automatism habits. To call such habits automatism habits is not to say that they *require* an absence of consciousness or volition for their exercise but only that such an absence does not inhibit the efficacy of the habit.

The distinction between mastery and automatism habits deepens our appreciation of Aristotle's odd claim that the clear-eyed incontinent acts "contrary to his choice" (1148a10). Since automatism habits may function independently of rational consciousness or volition, a person may act voluntarily and yet not act in accordance with his rational deliberation about how he ought to act. Following Aristotle, Aquinas offers the following picturesque metaphor of the relationship between reason and the automatism habits of the sensory powers: "The reason, in which resides the will, moves, by its command, the irascible and concupiscible powers, not, indeed, *by a despotic sovereignty*, as a slave is moved by his master, but by a *royal and politic sovereignty*, as free men are ruled by their governor, and can nevertheless act counter to his commands. Hence both irascible and concupiscible can move counter to the will: and accordingly nothing hinders the will from being moved by them at times" (1-2.9.2). In other words, the will cannot simply demand straightway that the

---

[1]George Klubertanz, *Habits and Virtues: A Philosophical Analysis* (New York: Appleton-Century-Crofts, 1965), p. 95.

appetites conform to its specification. The will can, and often does, override those appetites, and the will can effect the gradual transformation of those appetites through creative and intentional intervention, but at any given time the appetites may have habitual tendencies that are not directly translated from the will.

This metaphor of the relationship between rational and sensible appetites is strikingly confirmed by contemporary neurological research. For instance, William Irvine states:

> Our brains have not one center of control, not one part that wills, but multiple decision-making centers that independently come to decisions about what we should be doing with ourselves. They are like army generals who each has his own idea about what the battle plan should be. In most armies, a supreme commander listens to his generals' ideas and decides what should be done, thereby coordinating their behavior. But if a general is unable to communicate with the supreme commander, he might initiate a combat action on his own—an action that might be at odds with the actions of the other generals and with the battle plan set forth by the supreme commander.[2]

With respect to each action taken singly, the agent is always in a position to override automatism habits, but this does violence to agency and depletes the limited power of an embodied will. If the agent relents, the automatism habit does not. It acts "freely" against the orders given by deliberated judgment just as a free person can at times act in opposition to the demands of his or her political sovereign. Will and intellect exert lasting control over our sensory appetites only indirectly, by gradually modifying the judgments embodied in habits of the cogitative estimation.

The nondespotic control of reason over the sensory appetites leads Aristotle to emphasize again the way in which actions that flow from automatism habits are nevertheless voluntary. We have direct

---

[2]William Irvine, *On Desire: Why We Want What We Want* (Oxford: Oxford University Press, 2006), p. 95.

control only over our immediate actions, but because habits of action and passion follow in the wake of the repetition of certain actions, we can be held responsible for the actions elicited from these habits: "Actions and states of character are not voluntary in the same way; for we are masters of our actions from the beginning right to the end, if we know the particular facts, but though we control the beginning of our states of character the gradual progress is not obvious, any more than it is in illnesses; because it was in our power, however, to act in this way or not in this way, therefore the states are voluntary" (1114b30-1115a3).

If we apply Aristotle's and Aquinas's category of habit to addiction, we are able to see how it could simultaneously be true that an addicted person loses direct control over his choices yet remains in some sense able to respond to that loss of direct control. This opens up a way of resolving the addiction paradox—the seemingly contradictory claim that acknowledging lack of control is the first step toward regaining control over addictive behavior. For addicted persons do indeed lack the resources necessary to exercise enduring control over their addictive behavior but nevertheless possess the resources to act *indirectly* in such ways as to eventually develop the habits needed to make such enduring control a reality. Thus there is nothing philosophically incoherent in A.A.'s approach, which claims that addicted persons lack immediate control over their behavior and yet can regain that control in a nonmedicalized context.

Addiction, then, should be understood as a complex habit, and the "baffling" aspects of addictive behavior become less so as we gain a deeper appreciation of the myriad ingredients that factor into the functioning of a complex habit. Once we see that the relationship between a complex habit and the deliberative will is oblique and indirect, the recalcitrance of addictive behavior even in the face of "willpower" and "common sense" becomes intelligible.

If addiction is appropriately defined as a complex habit, what follows from this? The analysis thus far has shown that the category of habit provides a way of thinking about addiction that avoids the disease/choice dichotomy. It has also shown that thinking about addiction as habit does indeed give us tools for thinking about some of the more perplexing elements of addictive behavior. But I think the descriptive and explanatory power of the category of habit with respect to addiction can be extended. The way to extend the investigation in further fruitful directions is by now asking about the *kind* of complex habit that addiction is. Which powers of the human person are implicated in the habit of addiction, and most important, what are the goods to which the habit of addiction is directed?

ADDICTION AND INTEMPERANCE

As we seek to understand the kind of habit that addiction is, an obvious starting point is the habit of temperance. Perhaps addiction can be understood straightforwardly as a failure of the virtue of temperance, particularly as an expression of the vice of intemperance.

"Temperance," Aristotle tells us, "is a mean with regard to pleasures" (1117b24). But temperance is not concerned with pleasure in general, rather with pleasures of the body. Those who take excessive delight in pleasures of the soul, "such as love of honour and love of learning," are neither called intemperate nor self-indulgent (1117b27-32). Furthermore, temperance is not concerned with every sensible pleasure, "for those who delight in objects of vision, such as colours and shapes and painting, are called neither temperate nor self-indulgent," even though it is possible to delight in these things to an excessive or deficient degree (1118a3-7). Temperance is fundamentally concerned with the pleasures that human beings share with animals, namely those of touch and taste, but it is especially concerned with these pleasures as they are enjoyed "in the case of food and in that of drink and in that of sexual intercourse" (1118a31-33).

Temperance is, therefore, the virtue that enables a person to achieve proportionate desire and activity with respect to food, drink (by which Aristotle means mainly intoxicants) and sex. As already mentioned, the virtue of temperance resides substantially in the sense appetite and formally in the intellectual power. Temperance is a virtue necessary for the good life because the sensible appetite is not in itself rational. Insofar as human persons are rational creatures and the good life is a life in accordance with reason, the sensible appetites must be made to conform to reason: "Since, however, man as such is a rational being, it follows that those pleasures are becoming to man which are in accordance with reason. From such pleasures temperance does not withdraw him, but from those which are contrary to reason" (2-2.141.1). Temperance is the virtue that achieves this conforming of sense appetite to reason.

Three species of temperance correspond to the three objects of temperance: food, intoxicating drink and sex. Abstinence is the name of the specific virtue of temperance that denotes right moderation with respect to food; sobriety with respect to intoxicating drink; and chastity with respect to sex. A person can lack these virtues by either excessively or deficiently desiring and pursuing each of these sensible goods. Both extremes count as vice although deficient desire with respect to any of these sensible goods is so rare that it does not bear a recognizable name. Aristotle says that the person who deficiently desires and pursues food, drink or sex is "insensible."[3] Frigidity about sex would probably represent the most common form of insensibility. But, as Aristotle says, "people who fall short with regard to pleasures and delight in them less than they should are hardly found; for such insensibility is not human" (1119a5-7). The extreme of excess is the commoner vice, so common indeed that it has an accepted name with respect to each of the objects of sensory desire. Excessive desire and pursuit of food is called gluttony; of intoxicating drink, drunkenness; and of sex, lust.

---

[3] According to Aquinas, "If a man were knowingly to abstain from wine to the extent of molesting nature grievously, he would not be free from sin" (2-2.150.1). Stanley Hauerwas has mentioned to me the similar saying of the rabbis that "God will not hold him guiltless who has not enjoyed every legitimate pleasure."

If addiction is to be assimilated to the vice of intemperance, it will most likely be because of a substantial correlation between addiction and the vice of drunkenness. The vice of drunkenness can be understood as habitually excessive desire and pursuit of the sensible pleasures associated with intoxicants, which pleasures are overvalued as being suitable to the good life. For addiction to fit this bill, we should be able to describe addiction as *habitually excessive desire and pursuit of the sensible pleasures associated with certain intoxicating objects, which pleasures are overvalued as being suitable to the good life.*

Does this description do justice to the phenomenon of addiction? I submit that it does not for the following reason: Intemperance is the inordinate love of certain objects because of the sensory pleasures they provide whereas addiction is the inordinate love of certain objects for reasons other than sensory pleasure. In fact, persons may be addicted to a substance even in the *absence* of sensory pleasures and sometimes in the face of strong sensory *aversions* to the object.

Recall, for instance, the testimony of the clear-eyed incontinent alcoholic reported in chapter two: "I *knew* I would start working on the half gallon again, despite the fact that I was still very ill from the night before. I also knew that I did not want to drink. Sitting on that sofa, I realized that the old 'I could stop if I wanted to, I just don't want to' didn't apply here, because I did not want to drink. I watched myself get up off the sofa and pour myself a drink" (AA 324). Similar reports constantly appear in the memoirs of other addicted persons. These testimonies cut to the core of the experience of addiction. They could not be made by intemperate drinkers who simply love to drink too much. Even formerly intemperate drinkers who are working to overcome their intemperance could not report that they lacked desire for alcohol; they could only report that they wished they did not desire alcohol as they do.

In the addiction literature, this phenomenon is called "ambivalence." It is characterized by a mixture of desire for and aversion to the addictive object. How is it possible for a person to simultaneously desire and detest one and the same object? Offering a response to this question will enable us to better grasp the difference between intemperance and addiction. Aquinas says: "The appetite is twofold, namely the sensitive, and the intellective which is called the will. The object of each is the good, but in different ways: for the object of the sensitive appetite is a good apprehended by sense, whereas the object of the intellective appetite or will is good under the universal aspect of good, according as it can be apprehended by the intellect" (1.80.2). Simply put, the objects of the sensitive appetite are the goods of sensory pleasures whereas the objects of the intellective appetite are other sorts of goods, intellectual or moral goods for example.

We recall that intemperance is a habit substantially of the sensitive appetite. Therefore, if addiction is to be successfully assimilated to the habit of intemperance, we should find that it has primarily to do with an inordinate desire for certain sensory pleasures associated with addictive objects. But although many addictions find their infancies in the enjoyment of sensory pleasures associated with the addictive object, advanced addiction is rarely concerned with sense pleasures. Take, for example, the following testimonies.

> A group of colleagues had piled into a car to drive somewhere for lunch. I was last and sat squeezed in among several others on the back seat. An acquaintance had lit a cigarette which was beginning to upset my stomach. I started to ask him to roll down the window. But he immediately opened it and threw out the cigarette. I said something like, "I'm sorry to spoil your pleasure." He replied decisively, "It's not pleasure, it's smoking."[4]

---

[4]Bruce Wilshire, *Wild Hunger: The Primal Roots of Modern Addiction* (Lanham, Md.: Rowman and Littlefield, 1998), p. 145.

Certainly drinking was no longer fun. It had long ago ceased to be fun. A few glasses of wine with a friend after work could still feel reassuring and familiar, but drinking was so need driven by the end, so visceral and compulsive, that the pleasure was almost accidental. Pleasure just wasn't the point.[5]

These addicted persons are not driven by the pursuit of sensory pleasures. Such pleasures are said to be either beside the point or altogether absent. It seems much more likely, then, that the goods addicted persons pursue through the practice of their addictions are better understood as "objects of the intellective appetite or will." Nowhere is this claim more indisputably evident than in the frequent testimonies of addicted persons who formed an addiction, not through the gateway of sensory pleasure, but rather *in spite of* the manifest sensory misery occasioned by their earliest acquaintance with the addictive object. The following testimonies of three addicted persons can only sound grotesque to those who have not experienced the power of major substance addiction.

I don't remember how many drinks I had, and my recollections of the actual events of the rest of the night are fuzzy, but I do remember this much: When I was drinking, I was okay. I understood. Everything made sense. I could dance, talk, and enjoy being in my own skin. It was as if I had been an unfinished jigsaw puzzle with one piece missing; as soon as I took a drink, the last piece instantly and effortlessly snapped into place. . . . I recall thinking, as I knelt retching in the stall, that this was fantastic. Life was great; I had finally found the answer—alcohol! (AA 320)

Everything changed with my first drink at the age of sixteen. All the fear, shyness, and disease evaporated with the first burning swallow of bourbon straight from the bottle during a liquor cabinet raid at a slumber party. I got drunk, blacked out, threw up, had dry heaves, and was sick to death the next day, and I knew I would do it again.

---

[5]Caroline Knapp, *Drinking: A Love Story* (New York: Dial Press, 1996), p. 210.

For the first time, I felt part of a group without having to be perfect to get approval. (AA 328)

I took to dope from the start, but many people who later become junkies will tell you that the first time, or two times, or even every time they got high, they threw up. Would you order an entrée again if you threw up the first time you ate it? Would you go out on cold nights to dubious streets to buy it? Risk arrest?[6]

Loss of memory, blackouts, vomiting, dry heaves and being deathly ill are not normally counted among the variety of sensory pleasures. Yet these addicted persons pursue their addictive objects because those objects are believed to offer definite goods, goods like the ability to communicate, being at ease with oneself, being unafraid and being part of a community. These goods seem more like objects of the intellective rather than the sensitive appetite; they are types of moral and intellectual goods.

Major addiction, therefore, simply does not fit the bill of intemperance, which has to do with the pursuit of sensory pleasures of taste and touch. Put simply, intemperance may be understood as a form of hedonism, whereas addiction cannot. Indeed, the life of the addicted person would seem appalling to one who was set on maximizing immediate sensory gratification. The experienced intemperate drinker will in fact *moderate* his alcohol consumption, although the "mean" he seeks is one determined by a kind of sensory pleasure calculus rather than, as in the case of the temperate drinker, prudential deliberation about the life of human flourishing. However, the alcoholic knows no moderation, even though he may know that moderation could in fact increase his strictly sensory pleasure, at the very least by preventing the variety of sensory miseries that the inveterate alcoholic endures.

It is because addiction is not concerned with sensory pleasures but rather with intellective goods that addicted persons are commonly

---

[6]Ann Marlowe, *How To Stop Time: Heroin from A to Z* (New York: Basic Books, 1999), p. 145.

ambivalent about their drug of choice. The ambivalence is made possible by the abstract nature of intellective goods. The alcoholic can think of a whiskey as good in one way, bad in another: good for drowning loneliness, good for summoning courage and so on (moral goods, all); bad for spiritual well-being, bad for relationship to spouse and so on (moral ills, all). But the intemperate drinker thinks of a beer only in terms of pleasure, which, as a concrete good, is not susceptible to contrary interpretations. Bad pleasure is, strictly speaking, an oxymoron. The crucial difference between intemperance and addiction, therefore, lies in the different sorts of goods that each pursues. Intemperance pursues sensory goods; addiction pursues moral and intellectual goods.

Because the goods pursued through the practice of addictions are moral and intellectual whereas the goods pursued through intemperate behavior are sensory, addicted and intemperate persons respond differently to shame and guilt. Aquinas counts "shamefacedness" as one of the two integral "secondary virtues" or sub-virtues of the virtue of temperance, along with *honestas*, a sense of moral beauty or decorum, the violation of which provokes the response of shamefacedness (2-2.143.1). Shamefacedness "is the fear of something base, namely of that which is disgraceful" (2-2.144.1). Aquinas says that intemperance is held in check exactly to the extent that an agent feels ashamed of his intemperate behavior. Thus an inverse relationship holds between shame and intemperance: the more pronounced the experience of shame, the less pronounced the temptation to intemperate action.

But, in the case of addiction, we see precisely the opposite relationship between shame and addictive behavior. For persons with addictions, shame is not a check on addictive behavior but rather an impetus to it. Shame and guilt are moral deficiencies that, in the addictive mind, can be redressed through addictive behavior. Describing the self-defeating character of an addict's shame and guilt, William Cope Moyers writes: "Shame and guilt grew. My self-esteem disappeared. Cocaine and beer tempered these emotions. I began feeling shame. I had no self-esteem. . . . I turned to the only help I thought there was—beer and cocaine."[7] Because the need underlying addictive behavior is a moral and intellectual need, the pain of shame and guilt merely compounds a sense of moral and intellectual lack. Recovering heroin addict William Pryor explains: "It is progressive because addiction feeds on itself, because the precursor pain has been subsumed into the pain of addiction, and the greater that pain, the greater the quantity of stuff needs to be taken, causing greater pain."[8] The more an addicted person uses, the more shame and guilt he feels. The original pain is compounded by pain of shame and guilt, and the addicted person uses more to numb himself to the pain.

If addiction is not to be assimilated to the vice of intemperance, this is because addiction does not seem to be essentially concerned with those goods with which the virtue of temperance is concerned, nor is it a response to the same kind of need that motivates intemperate action. But the testimonies of persons with addictions make plain that addiction is powerfully rooted in the pursuit of certain goods, goods that appear to addicted persons to be uniquely accessible through the practice of their addictions.

Addictions are like virtues and vices in this respect, since virtues and vices are habits that empower persons to pursue consistently, successfully and with ease various kinds of goods. Put simply, virtues and vices are those habits through the practice of which human beings aim at the good life, the life of happiness or, in Aristotle's terminology, the life of *eudaimonia*. Vices differ from virtues not by the formal role they play in the lives of moral agents but simply by whether or not they enable a person to achieve a life of genuine *eu-*

---

[7]William Cope Moyers with Katherine Ketcham, *Broken: My Story of Addiction and Redemption* (New York: Viking, 2006), p. 147.

[8]William Pryor, *Survival of the Coolest: An Addiction Memoir* (Bath, U.K.: Clear Press, 2003), p. 213.

daimonia. In other words, the virtuous person differs from the vicious person, not because one aims at *eudaimonia* and the other does not, but because one in fact advances into the life of *eudaimonia* and the other does not. As Aquinas helpfully puts it, vicious persons are those who "turn from that in which their last end *really* consists: but they do not turn away from the intention of the last end, which intention they mistakenly seek in other things" (1-2.1.7, my emphasis). Wherever we have habits of passion and action that connect with an agent's intention of the good life for human beings, we are in the realm of the habits of virtue and vice. And, as the excerpts above make plain, addictions are the locus of just such a connection. It therefore behooves us, as we try to articulate the type of complex habit that addiction is, to inquire more carefully into the way in which addiction may help an agent pursue or attain a variety of goods that are thought to be integral to the best possible life for human beings.

We are neither taught nor inclined to think of addicted persons as being actively and passionately engaged in the pursuit of the good life. We tend to think of them as persons who have checked out of the game or who are positively bent on destruction. But this is not so. I maintain that addictive behavior can tell us more than almost any other kind of human behavior about what human beings most deeply desire.

5

ADDICTION AND MODERNITY

The Addict as Unwitting Prophet

◆

Once there were no addicts. Or at least if there were, no one could have known it. The notion of the "addict" and the corresponding concepts of addiction and addictive substances are of modern vintage. The first recorded use of *addict* as a noun dates to 1899.[1] The contemporary notion of addiction is distinctly American in its ancestry. It was developed and refined in the crucible of the nineteenth-century temperance movement.[2] Responding to the increased social stigma surrounding drunkenness and the corresponding social pressure to abstain from alcohol, a number of Americans began to report that they experienced overwhelming desires for alcohol. The modern concept of addiction was worked out as a response both to these testimonies and to the exigencies of the burgeoning temperance movement. By and large, physicians carried out the development of the modern addiction concept, and it is in an article by Dr. Benjamin Rush, published in 1805, that we find the earliest description of "addiction" as a loss of control over the decision to drink.[3]

---

[1] *The Oxford English Dictionary* online, s.v. "addict."
[2] The seminal and most concise account of the genealogy of the concept of addiction is Harry Gene Levine, "The Discovery of Addiction," *Journal of Studies on Alcohol* 39 (1978): 143-74.
[3] Benjamin Rush, "An Inquiry into the Effects of Ardent Spirits upon the Human Body and Mind with an Account of the Means of Preventing and of the Remedies for Curing Them,"

But if there were once no addicts, today it is possible to believe that there is no one who is *not* an addict. Rush's formulation of the addiction concept was slowly assimilated into public consciousness and has since been buttressed and extended to cover an ever-growing catalog of addictions. Now, we all live in an "addicted society."[4] "Addiction is our way of life."[5] And, "major addiction is the sacred disease of our time."[6] Such a view of the ubiquity of addiction has become almost de rigueur in contemporary life, especially in America.

The numbers alone are staggering. Despite the avalanche of anti-tobacco education and advertising, approximately one out of every three Americans is addicted to nicotine in some form. Every year, nearly thirty-five million Americans try to quit smoking; less than fifteen percent succeed.[7] One out of every eight Americans is diagnosable with addiction to illicit drugs or alcohol.[8] Paradoxically, despite a decrease in total alcohol and narcotics consumption, estimates of the number of substance addicts in America have risen steadily over the last several decades. Increasing numbers of Americans are being prescribed treatment for addictions or are seeking treatment themselves. Additionally, medical establishments are expanding the scope of addiction at a rapid rate, regularly coining new addictions and thereby creating, seemingly out of thin air, vast populations of new addicts. Even those of us who have so far managed to avoid a definite diagnosis nevertheless tend to view our own behavior through the lens of the addiction concept. Thus we worry that we may be getting addicted to any number of things: what was once a sweet tooth is now a chocolate addiction; what was once a long day at the office is

---

reprinted in *Quarterly Journal of Studies on Alcohol* 4 (1943-1944): 325-41.
[4]Anne Wilson Schaef, *When Society Becomes an Addict* (New York: HarperOne, 1988).
[5]Stanton Peele and Archie Brodsky, *Love and Addiction* (New York: Signet, 1975), p. 182.
[6]Gerald May, *Addiction and Grace* (New York: HarperCollins, 1988), p. viii.
[7]National Institutes of Health-National Drug Abuse Administration, "Research Report Series: Tobacco Addiction," p. 3, www.drugabuse.gov/PDF/TobaccoRRS_v16.pdf.
[8]U.S. Substance Abuse and Mental Health Services Administration, "Substance Dependence, Use, and Treatment," www.oas.samhsa.gov/nsduh/2k7nsduh/2k7results.cfm#Ch7.

now workaholism; what was once lust is now sex addiction.

We all know that addiction is rampant in our day. But why? What exactly is it about our time or our culture that seems to make addiction itself such a compelling option and the concept of addiction such a natural way of interpreting and describing our behavior and experience? The remainder of this chapter unpacks the peculiarly modern roots of contemporary addiction by tracing the modern explosion of addictive experience and addiction language back to seismic shifts in social arrangements and worldview that accompanied the emergence of the modern way of life.

Recall that the burden of the previous chapter was to establish an initially counterintuitive thesis, namely that addiction *cannot* be analyzed as an extreme instance of the habit of intemperance. Whereas intemperate persons are driven by the pursuit of sensory goods, addicted persons are driven by the pursuit of moral and intellectual goods. Building on that insight, I contend in this chapter that addiction is ubiquitous in contemporary life, both as a type of behavior and as a way of conceptualizing behavior, because addiction makes accessible certain kinds of moral and intellectual goods, which the developments of modernity have made otherwise difficult to attain.

At first glance such a contention seems implausible because it suggests that addiction is an activity with constructive ends. But this is exactly what I shall argue. To make this argument, I return again to the thought of Aristotle in order to illuminate a stark break between premodern and modern ways of thinking about the moral life. Whereas premodern moral thought was characterized by a recurrent appeal to a robust and mutually held account of human flourishing, modern moral thought is characterized by a lack of any analogous shared context for envisioning the good life for human persons. Addiction, I contend, is the definitive habit of our time exactly because it offers the most powerful available response to this peculiarly modern lack.

ARISTOTLE ON HABIT AND HAPPINESS

According to Aristotle, "human good turns out to be an activity of soul in accordance with virtue, and if there are more than one virtue, in accordance with the best and most complete" (1098a17-19). Given this claim, one would expect to learn from the *Nicomachean Ethics* just what this "best and most complete" virtue is, but an incontrovertible answer is never supplied. Aristotle seems to offer two different answers to the question, answers that appear to be in tension with one another.

For most of the *Ethics*, Aristotle develops the view that the good life for human beings is realized through virtuous practical activities—activities like having a family, cultivating friendships and governing cities. Moral and intellectual virtues are developed through such practical pursuits, and growth in the virtues is constitutive of the good life. The virtues are constitutive of the good life both because they facilitate the practical activities of family, friendship and political life, and because they are worthwhile in their own right: "Now such a thing happiness [*eudaimonia*],[9] above all else, is held to be; for this we choose always for itself and never for the sake of something else, but honour, pleasure, reason, and every virtue we choose indeed for themselves (for if nothing resulted from them we should still choose them), but we choose them also for the sake of happiness, judging that by means of them we shall be happy" (1097a37-1097b5).

But in book ten of the *Nicomachean Ethics*, and also in the *Eudemian Ethics*, Aristotle changes gears and claims that the good life can be attained only through the practice of pure contemplation of the divine (*theoria*). Here Aristotle contends that the moral and intellec-

---

[9]"Happiness" translates the Greek word *eudaimonia*. Much ink has been spilled on the question of how *eudaimonia* should be translated. "Happiness" is probably not the best translation because it could be associated with a "whatever makes you happy" mentality, which was certainly not Aristotle's view. Aristotle thought you might be enjoying yourself and yet fail to be *eudaemone*. It is probably better translated by "the worthwhile life," "the life of flourishing," "the best possible life," etc., but I use these as well as "happiness" interchangeably.

tual virtues are in themselves insufficient for the attainment of happiness. These virtues and the practical activities that are entailed by them are to be ordered toward the ultimate goal of contemplating and serving God: "Therefore whatever mode of choosing and of acquiring things good by nature—whether goods of body or wealth or friends or the other goods—will best promote the contemplation of God, that is the best mode, and that standard is the finest; and any mode of choice and acquisition that either through deficiency or excess hinders us from serving and from contemplating God—that is a bad one."[10]

We can distill from these different pictures two questions that can be treated separately. First, if the moral virtues are in some way constitutive of the good life, how are they to be internally ordered toward the realization of such a life? Second, if contemplation of the divine is a necessary component of *eudaimonia*, how is this more transcendent aspect of the good life to be integrated with the practical exercise of the moral virtues?

These two questions set the trajectory for the remaining argument of this book. The first half of the book established that the language of habit is indispensable for rightly describing addictive action. The remainder employs the insight that addiction is habit to explore why addiction is such a predominant and powerful contemporary phenomenon. Although I have used questions that arise from Aristotle's *Ethics* to set the stage, similar questions arise within any attempt to state the meaning of human action. Is human action ordained to certain purposes and ends, to a specifiable *telos*? And, can human action lead us beyond the immanent plane toward some participation with that which is transcendent or divine? Aristotle and Aquinas are helpful interlocutors here because their answers to these questions differ so markedly from the answers provided by the dominant forms of modern thought.

---

[10]Aristotle, *Eudemian Ethics*, trans. H. Rackham, in *Aristotle: Athenian Constitution, Eudemian Ethics, Virtues and Vices* (Cambridge, Mass.: Loeb Classical Library, 1980), 1249b17-14.

My thesis in this chapter is that addiction can be interpreted as one available modern response to the lack of any common consensus about the *telos* of human action. The best way to see how impoverished a modern person is on that score is to explore the milieu of Aristotle, who wrote, by contrast, in an age when some things about "goodness" and the ends of human life could be taken for granted.

The political life of Aristotle's Greek city-state was tightly ordered around a shared conception of what such a political community must achieve in order to make accessible to its citizens the goods constitutive of a worthwhile way of life. And the *polis* was organized in such a way that these goods and the right ordering of them could be attained and achieved by excellence within a number of specific social roles and ways of life. Given a person's age, social class, educational background and such, there was widespread and collective agreement on the social role that a person should be pursuing or fulfilling, whether the life of artisan, military serviceman, statesman or philosopher. The citizens could recognize failure or success both at the level of political arrangement and at the level of individual endeavor because they shared a substantive conception of what sorts of practices and relationships were necessarily constitutive of a life of flourishing.

The ethical investigations that Aristotle carries out in the *Nicomachean Ethics* and elsewhere take as their point of departure this shared understanding. Aristotle does not attempt to establish from scratch a standard or principle of ordering that could radically question or reform this shared understanding. Rather, he seeks to unearth and state the philosophical assumptions about the nature of *eudaimonia*, which this shared vision already concretely embodied. Thus, for instance, when Aristotle frequently poses the question in the *Nicomachean Ethics*, "What do *we* say on such a topic?" he is not invoking the royal "we" as a polite form of rhetoric. Rather, as Alasdair MacIntyre explains, Aristotle asks "What do *we* say?" instead of "What do *I* say?" because he "takes himself not to be inventing an account of the virtues, but to be articulating an account that is implicit in the thought, utterance and action of an educated Athenian."[11]

The modern experience of addiction can be made intelligible against the historical backdrop of Aristotle's *polis*. In contrast to the Greek *polis*, modern social life is characterized by an absence of any widely shared account of the life of happiness. To use a popular term, modern social life is "pluralist" about the question of the good life for human persons; there is no mutually held answer to the question. If this is the case, then the question of the right ordering of the activities and other goods of life is a question that becomes explicit and intensified mainly in the modern context. To the extent that modern persons see themselves as moral agents confronting a variety of mutually exclusive ways of life, questions about the right ordering of the goods and activities of our lives become urgent and sharpened. Addiction, I contend, supplies a type of response to this crisis.

If I am right that the lure of addiction increases to the extent that we lack other intelligible means of ordering our lives, then we should expect addictions to gather around cultures or subcultures in which there is the greatest discrepancy between traditional ways of conceiving and ordering life and the contemporary possibilities open to those cultures or subcultures. Thus we should not be surprised to find that in America, for example, addiction is disproportionately prevalent on Native American reservations where few of the traditional modes of understanding and ordering the moral life remain and the possibilities that are on offer are in total discontinuity from these traditional ways.[12] According to the 2008 National Survey on Drug Use and Health, conducted by the U.S. Department of Health and Human Services, "American Indians" have the highest addic-

---

[11] Alasdair MacIntyre, *After Virtue: A Study in Moral Theory*, 2nd ed. (Notre Dame, Ind.: University of Notre Dame Press, 1984), p. 147.

[12] See Jonathan Lear, *Radical Hope: Ethics in the Face of Cultural Devastation* (Cambridge, Mass.: Harvard University Press, 2006).

tion rates (11.1 percent) by race in America.[13] Addiction researchers have attempted to trace such statistical disparities to differences in racial genetics. I propose, instead, that the prevalence of addiction is correlative to specific challenges that emerge wherever modern modes of conceiving the moral life are at odds with traditional forms of moral endeavor. To show this, I shall elucidate the connection between certain interrelated features of modern life—arbitrariness, boredom and loneliness—and the prevalence of major addiction in modern life.

MODERN ARBITRARINESS

I am not a historian, and inevitably my account of the differences between premodern and modern social contexts will be simplified. I am aware, for example, that the ancient context was *in practice* probably not as harmonious as Aristotle theorized (indeed, Aristotle himself was aware of this) and that the modern context *in practice* is probably not as fragmented as some of its critics suggest (and as some of its champions celebrate). Nevertheless, an Athenian reading Aristotle would have found him familiar, just as John Rawls, for example, seems to be describing more or less "our world." There is a radical difference between the two, and I think we have much to learn by stating the differences in stark terms.

Whatever contemporary Western society may be, it is not the Greek *polis*. Some critics of modernity bemoan this fact, and champions celebrate it, but at least on this fact both are agreed. How to assess "the modern" is a problem of enormous complexity, and just as there is not one "Enlightenment," neither is there one "modernity." We may nevertheless essay a generalization about modern life on which there is broad unanimity, whether the movement from the ancient to the modern is interpreted as an advance or a decline. The Greek *polis* was organized around a shared vision of the good life for

---

[13]U.S. Department of Health and Human Services, "Results for the 2008 NSDUH: National Findings," www.oas.samhsa.gov/nsduh/2k8nsduh/2k8Results.cfm#7.1.4.

human beings and a relatively rigid and hierarchical set of social roles into which persons were born or trained. The culture of modernity, by contrast, is characterized by the proliferation of visions of the good life for human beings and a resulting moral landscape in which human persons find themselves arbitrarily free to "realize" themselves in pursuit of one or several of an assortment of disparate "ways of life." And therefore, whereas the Greek *polis* was premised on the priority of the common good, modern culture is premised on the priority of the individual good. As Alasdair MacIntyre claims, "In Aristotelian practical reasoning it is the individual *qua* citizen who reasons . . . but in the practical reasoning of liberal modernity it is the individual *qua* individual who reasons."[14]

The shift that MacIntyre alleges is not the effect of a "top-down" philosophical decision to prioritize the individual over the communal. It is not as though someone suddenly decided that the individual should be determinative of the community rather than the other way around. Rather, the shift is the product of the disintegration over several centuries of any widespread consensus about the nature of human beings and their place in the world. The cast of characters in this historical drama is extensive: Columbus, Luther, Copernicus, Descartes and Kant are certainly among the major actors. But the transformation was not strictly or even primarily wrought among the intelligentsia. Throughout Europe and, later, in America, doubt took hold and festered at every level of society. What was in doubt, among other things, was the ultimate defensibility of any claim about the *telos* of human existence. The diminishment of widespread agreement on the matter was at first decried and later celebrated, but what *was* quite clear was that the meaning of the common good was being greatly attenuated. The decline of the *community* is correlative with the decline of what may be held in *common*, and so modern individualism is merely what comes in the wake of this cultural

---

[14]Alasdair MacIntyre, *Whose Justice? Which Rationality?* (Notre Dame, Ind.: University of Notre Dame Press, 1988), p. 339.

drama. Undoubtedly, this development has brought with it significant opportunities, but it has also made fertile ground for the emergence and growth of habits of addiction.

In her philosophically insightful addiction memoir *How to Stop Time*, Ann Marlowe makes an intriguing claim about addiction to heroin: "The biggest, darkest secret about heroin is that it isn't that wonderful: it's a substance some of us agree to pursue as though it were wonderful, because it's easier to do that than to figure out what is worth pursuing. Heroin is a stand-in, a stop-gap, a mask, for what we believe is missing. Like the 'objects' seen by Plato's man in a cave, dope is the shadow cast by cultural movements we can't see directly."[15]

It is precisely these cultural movements, so integral to who we are that they go unnoticed, toward which I am gesturing with the clumsy label of "modernity." However, Marlowe does not put the point quite as strongly as she could. For it is not merely that modern people find it difficult to "figure out what is worth pursuing." Rather, modern people are plagued by an axiomatic skepticism as to whether such a thing could ever be "figured out" at all, regardless of the effort expended. It is not that we cannot recognize viable ways of life. Rather, we confront an array of mutually incompatible options with the suspicion that there exist no rational grounds for choosing among them.

With the failure of the Enlightenment project to establish a purely rational and therefore universal basis for determining the normative structure of human life, modern people inherit fragments of past traditions' conceptions of the *telos* of human life without possessing an established way of deciding between these various visions. Ours, then, is a culture in which the decision to pursue one way of life at the expense of others can only be understood as an arbitrary choice, an existential assertion of the self in the absence of any ultimate ra-

---

[15]Ann Marlowe, *How To Stop Time: Heroin from A to Z* (New York: Basic Books, 1999), p. 155.

tionale. Modern persons no longer know what to do because they know all too well how many things they *could* do. One astute addicted person perceived a connection between his addiction and the threat of modern indecision:

> I realized suddenly that I had two diseases—the disease of addiction and the disease of Too Many Options. . . . What if I made the wrong choice? . . . I had always been afraid to make the wrong choice. I'd look at the two forks in the road and stand there for the longest time, worrying that one or both would lead me down the wrong path. Alcohol and cocaine helped me overcome the anxiety of indecision and the courage to move forward [*sic*], even if it meant rushing headlong down a crooked path and right over a cliff.[16]

According to Sean Desmond Healy, modern people, because of this tyranny of possibility, "lack a sense of purpose and drift around in a state of psychic doldrums waiting for a wind to come up to give them propulsion toward a destination that they themselves cannot identify."[17] Healy contends that no such wind is coming and thus modern persons are determined, like Vladimir and Estragon in Beckett's *Waiting for Godot*, to wait interminably. But this is not altogether so; addiction is such a propelling wind—though it is more like a hurricane. Addictive objects stand in for a rationally determinable *telos* because they are able to demand by other means—by means of addiction—a kind of absolute allegiance to a way of life that modern persons cannot attain through the exercise of rational inquiry into the best life for human persons.

Søren Kierkegaard's *Either/Or* provides the fullest expression of this modern loss of teleology.[18] What *Either/Or* isolated as the distinctively modern point of view was that which envisioned moral

---

[16]William Cope Moyers with Katherine Ketcham, *Broken: My Story of Addiction and Redemption* (New York: Viking, 2006), pp. 184-85.

[17]Sean Desmond Healy, *Boredom, Self, and Culture* (London: Associated University Presses, 1984), p. 74.

[18]Søren Kierkegaard, *Either/Or*, trans. Alastair Hannay (New York: Penguin, 1992).

and political debate in terms of a conflict between mutually incompatible and incommensurable visions of the life most worthy of pursuit. In *Either/Or*, the conflict is between the life of the aesthetic versus the ethical man, but the variety of possible standpoints is by no means limited to these two. What becomes characteristic of all such standpoints in Kierkegaard's modern estimation is the absence of any common criteria that could arbitrate definitively between various contenders for the worthwhile life. Thus, for Kierkegaard, choice is dislodged from the order of objective rationality and inserted into the order of subjective self-assertion. Given a person's age, social class, educational background and so on, we still know nothing that could help determine for the agent the life that she ought to pursue. Whatever form of life is finally pursued cannot be made intelligible as rational choice, but only as a Kierkegaardian "leap of faith."

As Hubert Dreyfus and Jane Rubin have argued, "Identifying oneself as an addict may well be an attempt to obtain the meaning once, but no longer, provided by the authentic commitments made possible by a traditional culture. . . . When someone says, 'My name is Joe and I am an alcoholic,' he is acknowledging an identity—that of an addict. . . . We believe that the reason that *addiction* has become the preferred mode of psychological and social understanding for so many people in our culture is that it removes their identity from the realm of arbitrary choice and establishes it as an incontrovertible given. . . . Addictions have become substitutes for commitments in our culture."[19] Or, as recovering heroin addict William Pryor saw, "Somehow being an addict answered my needs, my pain, *my lack of definition.*"[20]

Fyodor Dostoyevsky's "underground man" depicts brilliantly

---

[19]Hubert Dreyfus and Jane Rubin, "Kierkegaard on the Nihilism of the Present Age: The Case of Commitment as Addiction," *Synthese* 98 (1994): 6.
[20]William Pryor, *Survival of the Coolest: An Addiction Memoir* (Bath, U.K.: Clear Press, 2003), p. 3, emphasis mine.

the paralysis that confronts modern persons: "Obviously, in order to act, one must be fully satisfied and free of all misgivings beforehand. But take me: how can I ever be sure? Where will I find the primary reason for action, the justification for it? Where am I to look for it? . . . You know, ladies and gentlemen, probably the only reason why I think I'm an intelligent man is that in all of my life I've never managed to start or finish anything."[21] This picture of modern indecision may explain why *any* consistent commitment in modern society looks suspiciously like an addiction. Precisely because we doubt that anyone could have sufficiently compelling reasons to justify an unwavering commitment to a project or way of life, we can only interpret such commitments as disguised addictions. Since reason cannot compel, addiction is left as the best explanation. Because the connection between reason and will has been severed, the assertion of will can only appear addictive. Thus even for those who have not been diagnosed with an addiction, the language of addiction frames the interpretation of certain kinds of activity.

Ours is a contradictory culture in which the deep ambiguity about the possibility of justified commitment is matched in intensity by the ideologies of opportunity, self-realization and self-control. Addiction emerges at the point of impact between these contradictory impulses since it facilitates a single-minded pursuit of fulfillment in the absence of a rationale. Addiction, like existentialism, the philosophical impulse bequeathed by Kierkegaard and Dostoyevsky, is produced by a culture in which we are, at one and the same time, told to "Be all that you can be" and to "Have it your way." The collision of an ethos of self-realization with an account of human action that divorces freedom from teleology is the wreck called modern addiction.

But addiction is not the only available response to the modern loss

---

[21]Fyodor Dostoyevsky, *Notes from Underground*, trans. Andrew R. MacAndrew (New York: Penguin, 1980), pp. 103-4.

of teleology. The dominant response of our culture is simply to ignore the crisis by means of distraction. In particular, late modern capitalism provides consumers the opportunity to pursue "value" in the absence of any shared commitment to the good. Consumerism, therefore, distracts us from the paralyzing arbitrariness of modern existence by promising that we confer value on things simply by being willing to buy them. Thus consumerism is an expression of the wish to be distracted from the frightening prospect that we do not really know what is worthwhile. The pursuit of constant titillation, which is the pulse of consumerism, is the enthronement of the immediate over the teleological.

Addiction enacts a backlash against the notion of a self who consumes by arbitrary fiat of the will whatever seems to provide immediate gratification. Addiction is a sort of rejection of consumerism's enthronement of the immediate over the teleological. It is true that many addictions *begin* from a desire to be distracted by immediate gratification. But addiction is *addicting* rather than merely *distracting* exactly because it provides the kind of propelling and purposive force that consumerism cannot provide. Consumers buy and sell to distract themselves from a lack of purpose. But addicts find purpose at precisely the moment in which they recognize that, rather than consuming their products of choice, they are instead consumed by those products. Addiction provides what consumers do not believe exists: necessity. Major addiction can therefore be interpreted both as a response to the absence of teleology in modern culture and as a kind of embodied critique of the late capitalist consumerism which this absence has produced.

MODERN BOREDOM

We have been speaking of the need for distraction from a crisis of meaning. But to put the modern predicament in terms of a crisis of meaning, though true as a matter of fact, is misleading. It wrongly suggests that modern persons vigilantly seek resolution of the crisis, but this is not necessarily the case. For modern persons are not only plagued by the absence of a teleology but also by the belief that a resolution to the crisis is not forthcoming since the only imaginable sources of such a resolution—Aquinas's Faith, Kant's Reason, Hegel's History—are the very things that modernity has called into irremediable doubt. Modern persons, therefore, are not so much desperate as cynical or bored.

Ironically, with the disappearance of any widely held conception of a common good and the correlative transformation of the social sphere into an arena for individual projects of enjoyment and achievement, boredom ensued. It was Kierkegaard, too, who remarked that the root of what ails modern society is boredom: "Boredom is a root of all evil. Strange that boredom, so still and static, should have such power to set things in motion. The effect that boredom exercises is altogether magical, except that it is not one of attraction but of repulsion. . . . What wonder, then, that the world is regressing, that evil is gaining ground more and more, since boredom is on the increase and boredom is a root of all evil."[22] Lest it be supposed that boredom is a uniquely modern problem, we should remember that the early Christian church father Origen speculated that boredom caused the Fall.[23] But modern boredom is distinct from the "standard" boredom of old.

The material payoff of modern capitalism has meant that many modern people are freed from the daily struggle for survival and therefore that they have the problem of "spare time." Boredom, in the sense of not knowing how to occupy spare time, is the privilege of the relatively well-off, who because their energies are not expended on survival, must confront what to do with their time. As Aristotle remarked, "the noble employment of leisure is the highest

---

[22]Kierkegaard, *Either/Or*, pp. 227-28. Martin Heidegger also contended that boredom is the predominate mode of modern Being-in-the-world. See *An Introduction to Metaphysics*, trans. R. Manheim (Garden City, N.Y.: Doubleday, 1961).

[23]Origen, *On First Principles*, trans. G. W. Butterworth (New York: Harper and Row, 1966), 2.8.3.

aim which a man can pursue."[24] It is therefore of interest that Ro-
zanne Faulkner characterizes addiction as a "leisure malfunction,"
and proposes that training in how to spend leisure time well is fundamental to the process of recovery.[25]

But although capitalism has perhaps produced a larger class of
people with the "problem" of leisure time than any other social arrangement, the problem of leisure time is not unique to the modern
context, as is clear from Aristotle's concern with how it should be
well spent. The problem seems to run deeper, then, than the mere
fact that modern people have spare time. The problem in fact is that
the idea that one should spend one's leisure time in a "noble" way is
itself odd to modern people. Many modern persons have leisure, yet
they lack the ability to determine what would count for the noble
employment of it since they lack the ability to determine the kind of
people they should be and the kind of lives they should lead. Thus
leisure time is thought to be a time for hobbies or, more tellingly,
"diversions." How strange, then, to the modern ear that Aristotle
answers his own question, "What ought we to do when at leisure?"
with the response: "Clearly we ought not be amusing ourselves, for
then amusement would be the end of life."[26] For Aristotle, we only
know how to spend our leisure time if we know what our lives are for
and the end to which our lives are to be directed.

Because modern persons lack such a conception of what their lives
are for, their leisurely pursuits can only be efforts that may distract
from the crisis occasioned by such a lack. In other words, modern leisure can only instantiate rather than assuage the deep boredom of
modern existence. Thus I am wary of the facile suggestion that people
get addicted because they don't have interesting hobbies. One alcoholic describes himself as "father, husband, taxpayer, home owner . . .

[24]Aristotle, *Politics*, trans. Benjamin Jowett, in *The Basic Works of Aristotle*, ed. Richard McKeon
(New York: Random House, 1941), 8:3.
[25]Faulkner's work is cited in Bruce Wilshire, *Wild Hunger: The Primal Roots of Modern Addiction*
(Lanham, Md.: Rowman and Littlefield, 1998), p. 114.
[26]Aristotle, *Politics*, 1337b35-36.

clubman, athlete, artist, musician, author, editor, aircraft pilot, and world traveler." He seems to have no shortage of interesting hobbies and socially acceptable ways to fill his leisure time. But, he recounts, "There would be times when the life of respectability and achievement seemed insufferably dull—I had to break out" (AA 382).

This insufferable dullness—what Healy calls "hyperboredom"[27]—is uniquely modern. It is quite other than the boredom of earlier ages, which was characterized, according to Healy, by a disenchantment with one's particular place in the social schema. This "standard" boredom is seen as remediable to the extent that society as a whole is still believed to carry within itself the resources for constructing a worthwhile and meaningful life. But in the case of modern "hyperboredom," society itself is "under indictment for failing to provide meaning."[28] Listen again to the testimony of a modern alcoholic:

> The mental state of the sick alcoholic is beyond description. I had no resentments against individuals—the whole world was all wrong. My thoughts went round and round with, What's it all about anyhow? People have wars and kill each other; they struggle and cut each other's throats for success, and what does anyone get out of it? Haven't I been successful, haven't I accomplished extraordinary things in business? What do I get out of it? Everything's all wrong and the hell with it. (AA 225)

The absence of a shared or ultimately justifiable *telos* makes modern persons uniquely bored. Because one can do anything, there is nothing to do. It is not only, as in the case of standard boredom, that a particular way of life seems pointless. Rather, the search itself seems pointless, and therefore boring: "Hyperboredom" names the paralysis brought on by modernity's inability to justify one commitment over others.

---

[27] Healy, *Boredom, Self, and Culture*, chap. 3.
[28] Ibid., p. 61.

According to William Burroughs, "You become a narcotics addict because you do not have strong motivation in any other direction. Junk wins by default. I tried it as a matter of curiosity."[29] Given my argument thus far, Burroughs does not quite get to the heart of the matter, for one could take him to be saying that "junk" is one among many possible "diversions" that could have won "by default," as though some people who are bored take up golf and others take up "junk." Junk wins by default for a *reason*, and it is the reason that major addiction is the definitive habit of our time. Addictions provide compelling motivation toward specific ends in a way that is otherwise inaccessible to the modern person who can find no final criterion to justify activity in a definite direction. Burroughs gets much closer to the heart of the matter when he says, contrary to what we are led to believe about addiction, "the point of junk to a user is that it forms the habit."[30] If there is a uniquely modern disease, it is the dis-ease of modern boredom, for which addiction is one of the rare proven antidotes.

Modern boredom is not merely a bourgeois privilege. What is unique to the well-off is the way in which modern boredom is pressed on them in the crisis of leisure time. But modern boredom presses on those who are not so "burdened" with leisure time as well. These persons also live under modernity's shadow, and although their lives are filled with the daily grind of getting by, their struggles are accompanied by the constant question: What is it all for? As portrayed in Charlie Chaplin's classic film *Modern Times*, modern working-persons find themselves caught up in institutions and bureaucracies that use them like cogs in a machine. From the factory employee to the middle manager, modern workers are placed in roles that demand that they perform "act-fragments,"[31] insofar as the agent often has no conception of what the ultimate outcomes of her act might

---

[29]William Burroughs, *Junky* (New York: Penguin Books, 1977), p. xv.
[30]Ibid., p. 8.
[31]Wilshire, *Wild Hunger*, p. 13.

be, let alone any investment in the worth or meaning of those outcomes. The modern worker is busy, but she lacks purpose.

As the lives of modern persons are fragmented by the partitioning off of work from leisure, of the public from the private, of the religious from the secular, of the young from the old, of the local from the national, and so on, it becomes increasingly difficult to imagine how the activities and commitments of an individual life can amount to an ordered whole. Modern persons who are spread thin by their disparate and disconnected responsibilities desire some unifying principle that can supply integrity in the place of compartmentalization and fragmentation. The modern person, and in particular the modern working-person, is expected to pursue a variety of different activities with no overall good supplying any encompassing purpose or unity to life. The modern addict, by contrast, is a person for whom such heterogeneous goods can only appear burdensome because they are devoid of any connective thread. In the absence of such a thread, addiction offers a release from a welter of responsibilities that lack a unifying rationale.

Such a release may be sought, not out of sloth, but out of discontent. Thus, when Bruce Wilshire contends that addicts are people who "demand the rewards without doing the work,"[32] he puts the matter backwards. It is true that addiction in many ways stunts emotional growth and that addicts in recovery must learn the discipline required to weather the inevitable challenges that every life, whether ancient or modern, must face. But modern addiction is only derivatively a demand for rewards without work, for it is rooted more fundamentally in the suspicion that modern work is without rewards.

To recap the argument, if some modern persons suffer because they cannot find good reasons to become entangled in the business of life, others suffer from a kind of entanglement that is nevertheless

---

[32]Ibid., p. 234.

rootless and without meaning. Addiction provides a response to both kinds of crisis. Addiction provides a response to the underwhelming life of boredom that plagues the bourgeois in its leisure time by making one thing *matter*. And addiction provides a response to the overwhelming life of boredom that plagues the working class with fragmented and compartmentalized striving by making *one thing* matter. For those who are bored with nothing to do, addiction stimulates by entangling and consuming; for those who are bored with too much to do, addiction disburdens by simplifying and clarifying.

MODERN LONELINESS

In addition to fragmentation and boredom, modern persons are plagued by loneliness. The alienation and loneliness endemic to modern individualism has been theorized and documented by intellectuals and social critics in several fields of inquiry. One thinks here of the devastating analyses of the young Karl Marx in his *Economic and Philosophical Manuscripts of 1844*,[33] or more recently of the sociological inquiry into American loneliness provided in David Riesman's *The Lonely Crowd*.[34] Charles Taylor contends that modern loneliness is the product of "industrialization, the break-up of earlier primary communities, the separation of work from home life, and the growth of a capitalist, mobile, large-scale, bureaucratic world, which largely deserves the epithet 'heartless.'"[35]

Whatever the complex origin of modern loneliness, one thing is clear: Lonely people make good addicts. As *Twelve Steps and Twelve Traditions* so simply puts it,

Almost without exception, alcoholics are tortured by loneliness. Even before our drinking got bad and people began to cut us off, nearly all

---

[33]Karl Marx, *Economic and Philosophical Manuscripts of 1844*, in *The Marx-Engels Reader*, 2nd ed., ed. Robert C. Tucker (New York: W. W. Norton, 1978).

[34]David Reisman, *The Lonely Crowd: A Study of the Changing American Character* (New Haven, Conn.: Yale University Press, 1965).

[35]Charles Taylor, *Sources of the Self: The Making of the Modern Identity* (Cambridge, Mass.: Harvard University Press, 1989), p. 292.

of us suffered the feeling that we didn't quite belong. Either we were shy, and dared not draw near others, or we were apt to be noisy good fellows craving attention and companionship, but never getting it—at least to our way of thinking. There was always that mysterious barrier we could neither surmount nor understand. (TT 57)

The connection between loneliness and alcohol addiction is illustrated almost ad nauseam in the "Personal Testimonies" of A.A.'s Big Book. It is by far the most common theme. We have already heard from some. Here is a sampling of several more.

I had never been inside a bar until one evening some fellow students persuaded me to go with them to a local cocktail lounge. I was fascinated. . . . It was pure sophistication. . . . But more important than anything else that night, I belonged. I was at home in the universe; I was comfortable with people. . . . Not only was I completely at ease, but I actually loved all the strangers around me and they loved me in return, I thought, all because of this magic potion, alcohol. What a discovery! What a revelation! (AA 447)

Whatever the problem, I soon found what appeared to be the solution to everything. . . . A stop at a local bar began the evening. I ordered a beer from the waitress and as I took the first sip, something was immediately different. I looked around me, at the people drinking and dancing, smiling and laughing, all of whom were much older than I. Suddenly, I somehow felt I belonged. (AA 282)

Although I wasn't too thrilled with the taste, I loved the effects. Alcohol helped me to hide my fears; the ability to converse was an almost miraculous gift to a shy and lonely individual. (AA 359)

In her biography of Bill Wilson, the cofounder of Alcoholics Anonymous, Susan Cheever reports that Wilson's own addiction to alcohol was fueled by this thirst for companionship: "He never forgot the warmth of the tavern and the way the men there seemed to melt together into one person—a person immune to loneliness."[36]

---

[36]Susan Cheever, *My Name Is Bill* (New York: Simon & Schuster, 2004), p. 39.

Sadly, the search for belonging that finds its answer for so many alcoholics in the fellowship of the bar eventuates in near-total isolation. Alcohol, once the elixir of conviviality and camaraderie, is a jealous friend: "From that first night at the bar a year earlier, I had made a profound decision that was to direct my life for many years to come: Alcohol was my friend and I would follow it to the ends of the earth. . . . Now alcohol had become the only friend I had" (AA 447). Solitary drinking or use becomes the tragically ironic pinnacle of major addiction.

In an article on the difference between the preindustrial experience of "chronic drunkenness" and that of contemporary alcohol addiction, Peter Ferentzy makes the fascinating observation that before the turn of the eighteenth century solitary drunkenness was rare.[37] Yet this alarming fact becomes intelligible when we see that the modern rejection of teleology and the resulting loss of a shared conception of the good life for human beings entailed a transformation of the nature of friendship. For, as is so clear in the *Nicomachean Ethics*, friendship was for Aristotle a basically moral undertaking, with the relationship of true friendship defined primarily in terms of common goals and a shared pursuit of certain specified goods. For Aristotle, the primary benefit of friendship is not affection but growth in virtue. But this Aristotelian view of friendship has diminished along with the disappearance of a common good. It no longer seems appropriate to expect that friends will agree with one another about the more substantive matters of life. Now friendship is viewed primarily as an expression of affection (what Aristotle would have called a friendship of pleasure) or an exercise of career positioning and "networking" (what Aristotle would have called a friendship of utility) (1157b37-1158a3). For Aristotle, neither of these forms of friendship are true friendship because they lack any necessary connection to a person's growth in virtue and attainment of a life worthy of human beings.

---

[37]Peter Ferentzy, "From Sin to Disease: Differences and Similarities Between Past and Current Conceptions of Chronic Drunkenness," *Contemporary Drug Problems* 28 (2001): 382.

Addiction offers a twofold response to the loneliness implicit in the modern transformation of friendship. On the one hand, to the extent that affection and "social capital" mediate modern friendships, addictive substances lubricate this mediation, as many of the testimonies above have shown. Indeed, probably more than any other factor, it is the capacity of addictive substances to evoke strong affections or repress strong disaffections that represents their most immediate appeal. Under the influence of addictive substances, many people feel more free to express affection and more confident that they are receiving it.

On the other hand, precisely because addiction is able to supply an animating and necessary purpose otherwise inaccessible to thoroughly modern persons, persons with addictions do, in a sense, share with one another an unqualified and unconditional allegiance to a common goal. Addicted persons often find it hard to develop meaningful relationships with nonaddicted persons, and in this respect they are more Aristotelian than modern. Similarly, persons with addictions are more Aristotelian than modern in that they are willing to terminate friendships whenever those friendships inhibit their singular pursuit. Eventually, then, most addicted persons end up as they started—alone. Yet the solitary addicted person often finds that although she is alone, she is not lonely. This is because the addictive object itself takes on the role of friend and companion.

> When you're drinking, liquor occupies the role of a lover or a constant companion. It sits there on its refrigerator shelves or on the counter or in the cabinet like a real person, as present and reliable as a best friend.[38]

> I was never lonely when I was using, even when I was separated from the people I loved most in the world, because my best friends were always with me. Cocaine was my running buddy, my soul mate, my faithful lover, my reliable colleague, my fun-loving playmate who

---

[38]Caroline Knapp, *Drinking: A Love Story* (New York: Dial Press, 1996), p. 96.

tagged along everywhere I went. Alcohol and cocaine were always there for me, they never let me down.[39]

Ann Marlowe brilliantly expresses this aspect of addiction in her memoir.

> Like travel to faraway places, heroin served as a way of rendering my solitude beside the point. Doing it alone added no opprobrium; that was the least of my worries. And it made sense; the drug was a companion. . . . Being high allowed me to enjoy being alone without loneliness. . . . When I stopped getting high, what bothered me most was my relapse into loneliness, or into the awareness of it. . . . Dope made it easier for me to stay at home; dope was a home, a psychic space that filled the essential functions of the physical construct, providing a predictable comfort and security. Heroin became the place where, when you showed up, they had to let you in.[40]

To the extent that A.A. and other twelve-step programs are among the few places in contemporary society where, quite literally, when you show up they have to let you in, we begin to understand why intentional communities like A.A. are also among the few modern remedies for contemporary addiction. We will explore the relationship between addiction, friendship and recovery more extensively when we turn to the church's response to addiction. To wrap up this chapter, let me summarize what I have been arguing.

My intent in the foregoing analysis has not been to indict modernity by showing its horrible effects. Rather, my point has been to make intelligible the emergence and proliferation of addiction in modern culture, both as a form of behavior and as a mode of interpreting and describing behavior. I have tried to isolate those characteristics of modernity that I take to be the causes of this effect, contending that addiction supplies a powerful response to modern endemics of fragmentation, loneliness and boredom.

---

[39]Moyers, *Broken*, p. 185.
[40]Marlowe, *How to Stop Time*, pp. 140, 179.

Addiction is in fact a kind of embodied cultural critique of modernity and the addict a kind of unwitting modern prophet. The church has a great stake in listening to such unwitting prophets. If the church will listen, it will be led to an examination of how its own culture contributes to the production of addiction, whether it offers an alternative culture and what such an alternative culture would require.

6

ADDICTION AND SIN

TESTING AN ANCIENT DOCTRINE

◆

It used to be that we were all sinners in need of the grace of God. Today we are all addicts in need of recovery. For centuries, "sin" provided a description of the fundamental human predicament. Today "addiction" performs a similar task. William Lenters claims that addiction is "the human experience,"[1] and Gerald May proclaims, "We are all addicts in every sense of the word."[2] As May continues to describe the universality of addiction, the affinity between sin talk of old and contemporary addiction talk is striking. "Addiction, then, is at once an inherent part of our nature and an antagonist of our nature. It is the absolute enemy of human freedom, the antipathy of love."[3] Similarly, Christians have claimed that sin is at one and the same time part of our nature (the "sin nature") and yet antagonistic to what we are created to be.

If the language of addiction now functions analogously to the old language of sin, this is not because addiction is widely held to be synonymous with sin, or even a kind of sin. On the contrary, ad-

---

[1]William Lenters, *The Freedom We Crave: Addiction: The Human Condition* (Grand Rapids: Eerdmans, 1985), p. 11.
[2]Gerald May, *Addiction and Grace* (New York: HarperCollins, 1988), p. 4.
[3]Ibid.

dicted and nonaddicted persons alike have been taught to regard addiction as something fundamentally other than sin. Most addicted persons learn from their recovery programs and from a flood of addiction-recovery literature to be averse to the language of sin. Thus the recovering alcoholic is told that "alcoholism is a disease, not a disgrace,"[4] or the addicted person is told that addiction is "not sin but sickness." Addiction language, therefore, does not merely mirror the language of sin but is increasingly wielded to displace the language of sin.

The tendency within the addiction-recovery movement to either insist on a clear demarcation of addiction from sin or to replace the language of sin completely with that of addiction seems unpromising from a Christian perspective. Given that addiction is an ends-directed activity, it would be odd if an activity so destructive were entirely unrelated to sin. In addition, it seems unlikely that addiction can simply replace the concept of sin, not least because addiction is not in any obvious sense a theological category. How, then, should we understand the relationship between addiction and sin?

I have tried in the first several chapters to describe addiction in nontheological terms. In this chapter, we make a theological turn, attempting to set addiction in a definitively theological frame of assumptions about human nature and destiny. Just as I have contended that the classical category of habit can help us understand addiction better and describe addictive behavior more truthfully, I now want to contend that recourse to the concept of sin can similarly contribute to a fuller understanding of addiction. In fact, I will show that there are strong historical and conceptual connections between the philosophical category of habit and the Christian doctrine of sin. In order to pursue this strategy of relating addiction to sin, I first need to show that the standard argument that has caused reflection on addiction to be divorced from theological reflection

---

[4]From an A.A. brochure, quoted in Linda Mercadante, *Victims and Sinners: Spiritual Roots of Addiction and Recovery* (Louisville: Westminster John Knox Press, 1996), p. 6.

stems from a flawed understanding of what Christians mean when they speak of "sin."

SINS, SIN AND ORIGINAL SIN

The addiction paradigm is often presented as a critique (whether implicit or explicit) of the Christian doctrine of sin. This critique needs to be answered: Is there anything that we have learned from the study of addiction that would suggest that Christian anthropology, specifically the doctrine of sin, is inadequate or false? Only when this critique has been answered does it make sense to move forward and ask whether or not the Christian doctrine of sin may enrich our understanding of addiction.

Although the language of sin is largely absent from the Big Book of Alcoholics Anonymous, it does appear in the personal story of the cofounder, Bill Wilson. This is instructive because Wilson was at the center of a controversy within the ranks of A.A. about the propriety of employing specifically religious language within the A.A. program.[5] Wilson himself had been "saved" from his alcoholism by a religious conversion experience. In response to the testimony of an old school-friend who had been converted in a meeting of the Oxford Group (a lay revivalist movement that began in England and spread to America), Bill Wilson turned to God for help with his seemingly intractable alcoholism: "There I humbly offered myself to God, as I then understood Him, to do with me as He would. I placed myself unreservedly under His care and direction. I admitted for the first time that of myself I was nothing; that without Him I was lost. *I ruthlessly faced my sins* and became willing to have my new-found Friend take them away, root and branch. I have not had a drink since" (AA 13, emphasis mine).

Wilson's experience followed the pattern of conversion preached and practiced in the Oxford Group, and it was this pattern that be-

---

[5]For the history of A.A., see Ernest Kurtz, *Not God: A History of Alcoholics Anonymous* (Center City, Minn.: Hazelden Publishing, 1991).

came the template for what would eventually be the Twelve Steps of Alcoholics Anonymous. But soon after the formation of A.A., debate arose concerning how specifically religious language might actually deter A.A. from accomplishing its mission, which was to reach as many alcoholics as possible and to communicate to them a newfound method of recovery. Reference to "God" was permitted to remain, provided that it was always accompanied by the caveat, "as we understand him." Atheists and agnostics were encouraged not to allow such language to deter them from applying themselves to the Twelve Steps. They were invited to interpret God-language as the simple acknowledgment of some Power greater than their own willpower: "You can, if you wish, make A.A. itself your 'higher power.' Here's a very large group of people who have solved their alcohol problem. In this respect they are certainly a power greater than you" (TT 27). Thus God language was retained, but it was no longer necessarily tethered to the supernatural or transcendent.

Specifically Christian language, and particularly the language of sin, fell on even harder times. The complaints against such specifically Christian language were twofold. First, critics argued that alcoholics who were not Christian or who were averse to Christianity would be put off by it. Second, critics argued that religious language, especially the language of "sin," tended toward a moralism and voluntarism that was part of the very problem which alcoholics had to overcome, namely alcoholics' temptation to think that they could fix their own problem through straightforward moral exertion.

The doctrine of sin that most early A.A. members found too moralistic and voluntarist was the doctrine as it was presented specifically in the lay theology of the Oxford Group and more generally in the pre–World War II theology of an optimistic America. This theology was characterized by a strong emphasis on overcoming obstacles through the power of positive thinking. It denied that there were impediments to progress that could not be overcome through the exertion of willpower. As Linda Mercadante rightly points out, this is a variant of the fifth-century heresy known as Pelagianism.[6] For Pelagius, all sin is a transgression of a known law of God chosen by a will that is poised neutrally between good and evil, always perfectly and arbitrarily free to choose one or the other. Against Pelagius, Augustine argued that the human will is in bondage to sin, "not able not to sin," in his classic phrase (*non posse non peccare*). Augustine's reaction against Pelagius laid the groundwork for what has come to be the dominant understanding of sin in the Christian West. The language of sin that A.A. rejected was not the orthodox doctrine of sin as propounded by thinkers like Augustine. Rather, A.A. rejected a certain understanding of sin that had long since been found theologically wanting.

The church proclaims that sin is not fundamentally about human acts but about the human situation. The acts that we call *sins* are derivative of a deeper malaise called *sin*. In fact, we can identify three levels of specification within the doctrine of sin. On the surface, we have sinful acts, what have come to be known in the tradition, following Aquinas, as "actual sin." The apostle Paul tends not to speak of "sins" here but rather of "transgressions." Defining exactly what constitutes a sinful act is complex, but the standard definition is that a sinful act is any act that damages the agent's relationship to God.

At a deeper level, we can speak of the sinfulness of human persons. Most sinful acts do not come on the scene *de novo;* rather, they emerge out of our distorted character. Before most sinful acts occur, there is already a decided orientation away from God. This is called "dispositional sin" by Aquinas, and it is what the apostle Paul seems to mean when he speaks of the "flesh." "Sin" in this respect names not a type of act but a state, a situation or an orientation that a person as-

---

[6]Mercadante, *Victims and Sinners*, p. 116.

sumes. Thus, contrary to Pelagian thinking, a person can be "sinful" even if he or she is not engaging in some specifically sinful act.

This second level of sin develops as sinful acts lead to sinful habits, and these habits orient us away from God. Augustine's description of the way in which habit constrains our will is illustrative:

> The consequence of a distorted will is passion. By servitude to passion, habit is formed, and habit to which there is no resistance becomes necessity. By these links, as it were, connected one to another (hence my term a chain), a harsh bondage held me under restraint. The new will, which was beginning to be within me a will to serve you freely and to enjoy you, God, the only sure source of pleasure, was not yet strong enough to conquer my older will, which had the strength of old habit. So my two wills, one old, the other new, one carnal, the other spiritual, were in conflict with one another, and their discord robbed my soul of all concentration.[7]

Thus at the level of human sinfulness, the will is bound by its older willfulness, a willfulness that is produced by the formation of habits that orient the person in a definite direction away from God. Far from offering a voluntarist account of the human condition (as does Pelagius), Augustine's account of sin complicates our notions of voluntarity much in the way that Aquinas's category of habit complicated those notions. Augustine's account of the bondage of the will by habit suggests that this parallel between sin and habit is not merely coincidental.

But habit is not the only constituent of human sinfulness. For the doctrine of sin also maintains that, at the deepest level and prior to any habit-forming act, every human being finds himself already inclined away from God. This is what the evangelist John calls "the sin of the world" (Jn 1:29) and the apostle Paul refers to as the "sin that dwells within me" (Rom 7:18). Sin names a power or a force that

---

[7]Augustine, *Confessions*, trans. Henry Chadwick (Oxford: Oxford University Press, 1991), VIII.v (10).

bears down on every human person; every human person is a site for the exercise and influence of cosmic evil. Thus in every human person a tendency to evil precedes the exercise of will.

The Christian tradition has claimed that this is a truth about human existence that is known by faith. It is not the outcome of a particular argument or theory but rather an attempt to make sense of what Scripture says about the fundamental human orientation away from God. This factual claim has been theoretically explicated in a variety of ways. The apostle Paul seems to have conceived of this disorientation as the result of cosmological forces that vied from the outset against human fidelity to God. The Christian doctrine of the devil is therefore a correlate in some sense of this commitment to a force of evil that precedes human will. Additionally, Augustine argued for a doctrine of "original sin," which he claimed was transmitted biologically from Adam to every other human being in the form of a corrupted human nature. In the twentieth century, the social-gospel movement rejected this biological account of original sin and opted instead for an account of the social transmission of sinful structures and circumstances that await every human person and condition that person from the outset to be inclined away from God. However the claim is displayed, the Christian doctrine of sin includes a strong affirmation that prior to any sinful action, and therefore even prior to the formation of sinful habits, human beings are already predisposed to reject their calling to right relationship with their Creator. It teaches "that sin (at least since the Fall) is not in any simple way a *phenomenon* of, but is *prior to* individual freedom. Sin *pre-conditions* freedom."[8]

SIN, ADDICTION AND VOLUNTARISM

Contrary to the assumption of the addiction-recovery movement, the category of "sin" does not imply a moralist and voluntarist stance

---

[8]Alasdair McFadyen, *Bound to Sin: Abuse, Holocaust and the Christian Doctrine of Sin* (Cambridge: Cambridge University Press, 2000), p. 28.

about the power of human will. There is room within the doctrine of sin to recognize, as Augustine does, the bondage of the human will in the face of temptation. Indeed, the similarities between the doctrine of sin and the testimonies of addicted persons are striking. Persons with addictions claim that their addictive behavior is admittedly destructive yet, in some very real sense, beyond the immediate control of their willpower. Similarly the doctrine of sin teaches that human beings act in ways that are destructive of right relationship with God yet those actions often flow out of habits and fundamental orientations that are not amenable to reform through immediate exertion of will. We have seen that addicted persons do not merely perform certain kinds of actions but rather become certain kinds of people, and we have argued that habit is at least partially constitutive of this fact. Similarly the doctrine of sin claims that sinners are not merely people who commit sinful acts but are rather people whose character is sinful, and the role of habit is partially constitutive of this fact. Sin is therefore not fundamentally something that we *do* but rather something that we discover about who we *are*. Finally, persons with addictions claim that they are predisposed to addictions, that something about their material or psychological makeup inclines them toward addictive behavior prior even to the first addictive act. Similarly the doctrine of original sin teaches that sinners are not merely people who commit sinful acts, not merely even people who form sinful habits, but finally people who are predisposed to sin.

Thus the category of addiction is not in fact incommensurate with the category of sin, properly understood. Obviously some cases of addiction would not appropriately be classified as sin. For example, persons with severe mental illness are prone to addiction, but neither the language of habit nor the language of sin seems to rightly account for the dynamics at play in such cases. Rather, in such a case we would be more inclined to think of the addiction as both a disease and, in corresponding religious language, an instance of natural evil (rather than moral evil, or sin). But we have been trying to understand "incontinent addiction," instances of addiction that exhibit the "paradox of addiction." The majority of cases of addiction are cases of "incontinent addiction," and such cases of addiction are not incommensurate with the category of sin.

In standard cases of incontinent addiction—cases in which we rightly deem an addicted person responsible for his recovery, even while recognizing the limitations placed on his willpower—the category of sin is adequate to the dynamics in play. The paradoxical character of incontinent addiction consists of the fact that incontinent addictive behavior is at one and the same time voluntary and yet beyond the immediate control of a supposedly autonomous will. This is paradoxical because we are generally led to believe that the sphere of the voluntary is coterminous with the sphere of the autonomously willed—that one cannot be held responsible for something that one does not have immediate control over through the exertion of autonomous will. But I have argued that these two spheres are in fact not coterminous, and I have presented a philosophical category—habit—that can make sense of the disparity.

Similarly the doctrine of sin challenges the supposed symmetry between the voluntary and the autonomously willed. The contemporary addiction-recovery movement resists the category of sin, claiming that sin-talk simply reinstates the moralism and voluntarism that are the enemies of recovery. But in fact the Christian doctrine of sin, as articulated especially by Augustine throughout the Pelagian controversy, was developed and fine-tuned to resist precisely such moralism and voluntarism. The addiction paradox mirrors the paradox of sin: as Augustine argued, we may find ourselves unable not to sin and yet nevertheless rightly held to be acting *voluntarily* in our sinning.

The contemporary addiction paradigm, reacting against overly moralistic and voluntarist views of addiction, finds an ally in the disease concept of addiction. I have argued in the first several chapters of this book that, although the disease concept does provide a corrective to moralism and voluntarism, it does so at the expense of making unintelligible the actual modes of recovery that addicted persons successfully undertake. I have proposed instead that addiction be understood as habit, that philosophical category that mediates between autonomous choice on the one hand and determined disease on the other hand. Similarly the orthodox Christian doctrine of sin mediates between an overly voluntarist Pelagianism on the one hand and an overly determinist Manichaeism[9] on the other hand. It should, therefore, not be surprising to find that the language of sin may accommodate the experience and discourse of addiction.

The similarities between the controversies over sin that embroiled Augustine in the fourth and fifth centuries A.D. and the controversies today in the addiction-recovery movement are striking, but perhaps we should not be surprised. After all, both the ancient discourse of sin and the modern discourse of addiction are trying to make intelligible a certain kind of most paradoxical human behavior. It is no coincidence that both Augustine and addicted persons find their predicament paradigmatically stated in the words of the apostle Paul: "I do not understand my own actions. For I do not do what I want, but I do the very thing I hate. . . . I can will what is right, but I cannot do it. For I do not do the good I want, but the evil I do not want is what I do" (Rom 7:15-19). This suggests an important overlap between what the two categories— addiction and sin—are trying to describe.

This overlap can be misconstrued, however. It is tempting to conflate the two categories, such that sin is simply identified with addiction. Addiction is then taken to be the appropriate metaphor or model for all sin and is seen as a corrective to other faulty metaphors

---

[9]According to Manichaeism, the human person is little more than a battleground on which the opposed and independent cosmic forces of Good and Evil wage war against one another.

for sin, metaphors like "stain" or "transgression."[10] The shortcoming of this method, however, is that the language of addiction is privileged in such a way that we cannot even ask whether the doctrine of sin might also contribute insight to the discussion of addiction. If, as Patrick McCormick argues, "sin is an addiction,"[11] it is hard to see how this identification of the two categories can resist a reduction of sin to nontheological terms. The language of sin then becomes redundant. If sin is an addiction, and if we already know what an addiction is, then why even talk about sin?

The other way of misconstruing the overlap arrives at much the same result by a different route. Rather than conflating sin and addiction, the recovery movement in America has tended to simply dismiss the language of sin thereby denying the overlap altogether, confident that the language of addiction can stand on its own. Among other reasons, the recovery movement initially avoided the language of sin because sin was held to be a universal feature of human experience whereas the recovery movement wanted to emphasize the uniqueness of the addictive experience. What is interesting about this move, however, is that the language of addiction, in the theological vacuum created by the withdrawal of sin language, has been steadily expanded to fill the vacuum. This is the startling conclusion of Linda Mercadante who writes, "The thematic has thus come full circle. What was originally understood as the universal condition of sin, then reduced to the pathology of a particular group, and then expanded into a proliferation of addictive diagnoses has simply become another name for a universal human predicament."[12]

We must therefore be careful to avoid misconstruing the overlap between sin and addiction. The two categories can be neither con-

---

[10]This is the strategy pursued by Patrick McCormick, C.M., in *Sin As Addiction* (New York: Paulist Press, 1989).

[11]Ibid., p. 146.

[12]Mercadante, *Victims and Sinners*, p. 110.

flated nor entirely separated, and this can be shown simply by noticing the sorts of behavior that the two categories can cover. Many types of behaviors are instances of *both* addiction *and* sin. Drawing again on Aristotle's taxonomy of types of incontinence outlined in chapter two, it seems likely that most if not all cases of "simply incontinent addiction" are also likely cases of sin. In such cases, addiction is the result of a series of decisions made by an autonomous, competent and informed moral agent.

On the other hand, many instances of addiction are not appropriately labeled as sin. The example mentioned earlier of persons with a "dual diagnosis" of severe mental illness and addiction (cases of what Aristotle would have called "morbid addiction") would clearly be cases that cannot be interpreted as sin. Such cases are more appropriately interpreted in the category of natural evil. In addition, cases of addiction rooted in experiences of trauma or victimization cannot be placed straightforwardly into the category of sin. The overlap between sin and addiction here is extremely complicated. Although the victim cannot be held to account for becoming addicted, it does not follow that the category of sin is inapplicable to certain behaviors that may emerge from the addiction.[13] Yet clearly the category of sin cannot cover everything that is at stake in these situations. To adequately characterize such cases, as Cornelius Plantinga has suggested, we must resort to some broader category of moral evil such as "tragedy."[14]

Finally, many instances of sin are not appropriately labeled addiction. If a man rarely visits his aged grandmother in the nursing home because he is lazy or because he is put off by nursing homes, he is not obviously addicted but he is obviously under the sway of sin. These various cases suggest that, although sin and addiction

---

[13]See Christine Gudorf, *Victimization: Examining Christian Complicity* (Philadelphia: Trinity Press International, 1992).

[14]Cornelius Plantinga Jr., *Not the Way It's Supposed to Be: A Breviary of Sin* (Grand Rapids: Eerdmans, 1995), p. 139.

attributions overlap, the categories do not refer to an identical range of phenomenon.

What, then, is the relationship between the discourse of addiction and the discourse of sin? I have tried to show in this section that there is nothing described by the language of addiction that is in *contradiction* with what is predicted by the Christian doctrine of sin. Furthermore I have suggested that there is nothing *surprising* about addiction from the perspective of a robust doctrine of sin. The qualifier "robust" is important here, since the church always risks slipping into one or another impoverished and heretical views of sin, variants of Pelagianism or Manichaeism. The addiction-recovery movement has indeed been a highly constructive interlocutor as Christian theologians have sought to resist such defective accounts of sin and to rearticulate in contemporary terms the doctrine of sin. Yet I think it is fair to say that the addiction discourse does not bring anything that is genuinely novel to the Christian doctrine of sin.

So far I have shown only that speaking of incontinent addictive behavior as sin is permissible. But I have not shown that the language of sin is necessary or even particularly helpful in describing and displaying the character of such behavior. I have drawn attention to the way in which the Christian doctrine of sin can accommodate and even predict discontinuities between autonomous choice and voluntary behavior. This shows that sin language can accommodate even the most perplexing aspects of the phenomenon of addiction, but it does not show that sin language is needed to account for the phenomenon. After all, the discontinuities between the voluntary and the autonomous were shown in the first several chapters to be explicable by drawing on the philosophical category of habit. So far, then, there is nothing to prevent a rejection of theological language on the grounds that all of the "gains" of such language can just as easily be reached through a deployment of the category of habit, without all the additional religious "baggage" that sin language brings with it. The defense I have offered may justify Christians continuing to speak the language of sin in reference to addictive behavior, but it does nothing more than this. Such a modest accomplishment is all that could be expected of a defense of the adequacy of the Christian grammar of sin; to show more than this a different sort of investigation is now needed.

SIN AS A RELIGIOUS CATEGORY

Linda Mercadante has argued that the ascendancy of the addiction paradigm, particularly in America, is correlative to the attenuation of theological modes of reflecting on human experience: "The expanding application of the addiction metaphor is also a response to a theological vacuum created in part by the insecurities and resulting silences of religious communities as such core concepts as sin became unacceptable in public discourse."[15] Now we are in a position to ask: Given the displacement of sin language by addiction language, is anything lost? The answer is yes. The Christian doctrine of sin does provide explanatory and descriptive insight into the phenomenon of addiction, insight that is not accessible in the thoroughly naturalized terms of the addiction discourse.

I argued in the previous chapter that addiction is a peculiarly modern response to the loss of a compelling teleological view of human nature and activity. As Alasdair MacIntyre and others have argued, the loss of consensus in modernity about the purpose of human existence entails that the only "goods" on which we can all agree are the goods of survival and freedom from the incursion of others into our own private projects. A deviation or deficiency can only be characterized as deeply or profoundly as the "norm" with reference to which it deviates or falls short. Thus it should not be surprising that the secular discourse can only characterize addiction normatively as a deviation or deficiency insofar as addiction tends to damage our chances of survival and to restrict our free-

---

[15]Mercadante, *Victims and Sinners*, p. 107.

dom to pursue other projects that we value.

If our notion of the good and of human flourishing is restricted to normal physiological and social function, then our ability to characterize the destructive character of addiction will be similarly restricted. Moreover, such a restricted view of human flourishing gives those caught in the throes of addiction an impoverished sense of what they may hope for. Thus people are encouraged to battle their addictions in order that they may become "productive members of society." Alasdair McFadyen has argued that, in the absence of the eternal perspective implicit in the language of sin, we are not able to rightly characterize the "depth-dimension" of the most perverse "pathologies" that we encounter in the modern world. Speaking particularly of the "pathologies" of child sexual abuse and the Holocaust, McFadyen makes his point with persuasive rhetorical questions: "Is all that is damaged, distorted or lost through abuse normal physiological, emotional or social functioning? And is all that may be hoped for through therapeutic measures the return of those functions to a normal state? Is the depth of its pathology adequately captured if the holocaust is judged wicked on the grounds that it denied to millions of human beings the right to maintain life and avoid harm?"[16]

I want to make a similar point about addiction. We can only bring out the profound depth of addiction by placing it within a broader frame of convictions about human nature and human destiny. This means that the language of sin is not only *compatible with* the phenomenon of addiction but is also *necessary to* a characterization of addiction in all of its profoundly destructive power.

The category of sin is a religious category. Its central function is to speak of God and the world—specifically the world of human activity—in relation to one another. For, as McFadyen argues, "sin is an essentially relational language, speaking of pathology with an in-

---

[16]McFadyen, *Bound to Sin*, p. 201.

built and at least implicit reference to our relation to God. To speak of what damages human beings as sin is to claim that the essential character and defining characteristic of such pathology, however else it may be described and identified in nontheological languages, is theological: disruption of our proper relation to God."[17] Therefore, to speak of addiction in the language of sin is not simply to offer a moral or ethical evaluation of addiction, since the category of sin is not primarily a moral or ethical category. Rather to speak of addiction in the language of sin is to place addiction within a broader understanding of the nature of human desire and the ends for which human beings were created. When we speak of addiction in the philosophical category of vice, we draw attention to the way in which addiction constitutes a kind of moral deficiency, a disruption of the human person's pursuit of his natural or, in the language of Aquinas, "proximate" end. But when we speak of addiction in the theological category of sin, we draw attention to the way in which addiction constitutes not a moral deficiency but rather a falling away from our perfect good of eternal friendship with God. The emergence of the discourse of addiction was correlative to a loss of an agreed-on transcendent *telos* for human beings, but it points us back toward the need for such a language of transcendence in order to make sense of the phenomenon that the discourse is meant to describe.

---

[17]Ibid., p. 5.

7

ADDICTION AND WORSHIP

CARITAS AND ITS COUNTERFEITS

◆

Several years ago, a friend who had worked his way through graduate school as a paramedic told me about one of his more grisly experiences on the job. He received an anonymous call reporting that a heroin addict was on the verge of death in an abandoned apartment building. When he got to the apartment, the man was huddled in a corner, shivering and unresponsive, surrounded by piles of rotten trash, used syringes, lighters, spoons—all the paraphernalia of heroin addiction. When I asked what that experience was like, my friend related that it was terrifying, but that he also thought it was probably the first time he fully understood what worship looks like.

I have thought of this picture often as I have wrestled with the question of what addiction teaches us about our nature as human beings, and in this chapter I want to unpack the implications of my friend's insight that addiction is a kind of worship. In an effort to connect the categories of addiction and sin, I want to argue that addiction can be interpreted as a counterfeit form of worship.

Addiction is a complex habit. Like all complex habits, including what are called "virtues," addiction is a mode of human behavior that makes accessible certain kinds of human goods. Among these goods, addiction is particularly geared to the pursuit of certain moral and spiritual goods. Foremost among the moral goods that addiction pursues is an ordering principle for the exercise of practical rationality, and foremost among the spiritual goods that addiction pursues is an integrating principle that renders the immanent activities of human persons meaningful in light of some transcendent pursuit. This is my argument in a nutshell. The last claim about the relationship between addiction and spiritual goods remains to be vindicated.

If I can show that the phenomenological power and depth of addictive experience is most adequately displayed when we understand addiction as a counterfeit form of worship, then I will have shown how the language of sin deepens and extends our understanding of addiction. For all sin, as idolatry, is essentially counterfeit worship. All sin is the effort to attain independently of God that flourishing, integrity of self and delight that can only be attained through, that just *is* in fact, right relationship with God. Worship is our training in and enactment of that right relationship, and therefore those forms of human behavior that merely mimic the practice of worship and deceptively promise the fruits of right worship are expressions of human sinfulness. Thus to demonstrate that addiction is counterfeit worship is to demonstrate that addiction is sin and can only be adequately understood within the theological category of sin.

IMMANENCE AND TRANSCENDENCE

Worship, let us say, is right relationship with God. Worship is not restricted to the sanctuary or the prayer chapel, nor is it restricted to the morning "quiet time" or to bedtime prayers. Rather worship names the possibility that human persons may experience and live their days as an expression of their relationship with God. When we put the matter this way, we begin to see that worship is a mystery. Exactly what does it mean to prepare a meal or to mow the lawn or to take an exam as an expression of one's relationship with God?

To put the point differently, surely Paul is being impractical when he exhorts the faithful to "pray without ceasing" (1 Thess 5:17)? Obviously we have other things to do too. Yet the Christian tradition has always maintained that the calling and the privilege of the Christian is to live her entire life, in the words of Brother Lawrence, "practicing the presence of God." The call to right worship therefore raises a question: How are the immanent practices of daily life to be related to the transcendent quest for right relationship with God?

As we have already seen, the problem that this question raises stretches as far back as Aristotle. The *Nicomachean Ethics* is vexed precisely by a failure to relate these two dimensions of human life. In the first nine books of the *Ethics*, Aristotle argues that the best human life is to be achieved through the development of moral and intellectual virtues and the practical activities that these virtues facilitate—activities like raising a family, developing friendships and governing cities. But then, in book ten, Aristotle suddenly declares that the only activity truly fitting to the life of human flourishing is the practice of *theoria*, contemplation and service of the divine. Nowhere in the *Ethics* are we told how these two very different sorts of activities are to be ordered or integrated. As Thomas Nagel wryly comments, if in the end *theoria* is the only worthwhile undertaking, then it looks as though Aristotle believes "that human life is not important enough for humans to spend their lives on."[1] There is, then, a certain gap in Aristotle's account of the good life because he fails to explain how the life of practical action is to be integrated with the contemplation and service of God.

This gap in Aristotle's account of the life of human flourishing finds a definite response in the Christian thought of Thomas Aquinas. For it is Aquinas who provides a thick account both of the ways in which the life of practical activity is integrated with the human quest for the divine and of the means by which the various goods of human life may be rightly ordered to achieve this integration. The

---

[1]Thomas Nagel, "Aristotle on *Eudaimonia*," in *Essays on Aristotle's Ethics*, ed. Amelie O. Rorty (Berkeley: University of California Press, 1980), p. 11.

account that Aquinas gives is rooted in his account of the theological virtues—faith, hope and love. But his account leans most heavily on the theological virtue of love, which is the supernaturally infused virtue that capacitates human beings for participation in the life of God and thereby orders each of the other virtues to God. Aquinas's word for this virtue of love is *caritas* or "charity."

In order to pursue my thesis that addiction is a form of counterfeit worship, I want to explore the following question: What is it about charity that befits it to play this integrating and ordering role, and might addiction play a similar role? In other words, does addiction empower the addict to integrate the immanent and the transcendent in ways that mimic the function of the virtue of charity? My thesis is that the depth and power of addiction comes into full focus as we recognize how addiction is a counterfeit of the virtue of charity.

Obviously a Christian presupposition guides my argument, and it is simply the presupposition that there *is* a transcendent reality and that human persons have desires that are directed to that reality. There is no need for a vindication of such an assumption on Christian grounds since transcendence is a fundamental affirmation of Christian revelation. My argument could nevertheless be taken as a sort of indirect apologetic for such an assumption. For if addiction can be made intelligible as a strategy for integrating the immanent and transcendent in human life, then the overwhelming reality of addiction might suggest that an orientation to the transcendent is a fundamental feature of human nature.

The pre-Christian West was at a loss about how to integrate the human pursuit of immanent and transcendent happiness, and the Christian West claimed to supply an answer to this question. But the post-Christian world that we now inhabit is characterized by a suspicion or rejection of transcendence altogether. The post-Christian pursuit of flourishing and fulfillment, then, has been reduced to a project of immanence, and my argument will lend support to the thesis that addiction is a product of this modern privileging of immanence at the expense of transcendence. Addicts may be our most forceful and eloquent modern prophets, reminding us of the peril that a denial of the transcendent brings. So let us take a closer look at the theological virtue of charity, seeking to understand how charity institutes a link between the human pursuit of immanent and transcendent fulfillment.

AQUINAS ON CHARITY

Charity, Aquinas tells us, is friendship between human beings and God. It is a friendship based on God's communication of his happiness to human beings. More specifically, charity is "the love that is based on this communication" (2-2.23.1). Charity, for Aquinas, is grounded preeminently in God's movement toward persons rather than in persons' striving after God. Charity "is not founded principally on the virtue of a man, but on the goodness of God." It is therefore an "infused virtue," one for which human beings do not have a "natural" capacity (2-2.24.2). To speak of a virtue as "infused" is to point out that its realization depends on the work of the Holy Spirit; by an act of supernatural grace, God fills the longing soul with the love that draws the soul toward him.[2] Thus charity is a "supernatural virtue" because it directs persons to their supernatural end of fellowship with God. It is the strongest and most intense of all virtues, including the other supernatural virtues of faith and hope: "No virtue has such a strong inclination to its act as charity has, nor does any virtue perform its act with so great pleasure" (2-2.23.2).

---

[2]The language of "infused virtue" should not be confused with the language of "infused righteousness." The latter phrase pertains to the question of justification and highlights an area of conflict between Catholic and Reformation theology. Whereas Protestants have historically claimed that believers are accepted by God because the righteousness of Jesus is "imputed" to them as if it were their own, Catholics hold that believers are accepted by God because righteousness is "infused" within them as a gift of faith. The language of "infused virtue," however, addresses the theme of Christian sanctification. It is an attempt to describe how the process of sanctification entails genuine reformation of the believer yet remains at every step utterly dependent on God's prevenient movement toward human persons. To say that the change is "infused" is to insist that it is a gift of the Holy Spirit; to say that the gift is a "virtue" is to insist that it effects a genuine transformation in the believer's character.

How, for Aquinas, does the virtue of charity make it possible for us to participate in a relationship with God? After all, God is infinite and we are finite. We are not able to comprehend or understand God. How, then, can we love God? Moreover, how does charity integrate our practical endeavors into this relationship with God? After all, our practical pursuits and their corresponding moral and intellectual virtues are directed to finite goods whereas our pursuit of God is directed to an infinite good.

Aquinas answers these questions by proposing that charity is not in the intellective faculty but rather in the appetitive faculty. And the appetitive faculty differs, for Aquinas, in a very important respect from the intellective faculty: the appetitive faculty is infinite. Aquinas puts it tersely: "Rational concupiscence [desire] is infinite" (1-2.30.4). Each of us has longings that, according to Aquinas, cannot be sated by any finite thing. Paul Wadell explains the significance of Aquinas's position:

> If grace comes from God's side, desire comes from ours. Thomas grants that if we were finite in every way God could not be our joy, for we cannot "reach out to more good" than we can hold. But there is, he contends, one way we are not finite: we have unlimited desire. We are limited in every way but one—we have unlimited desire, unlimited longing. Our desire is the one thing about us that is not restricted and we know this. We feel the ongoing hunger for something infinitely good, we are stalked by the longing for something perfectly blessed and precious. Though we are limited, we want unlimited good, though we are restricted, we want to love unrestrictedly. . . . This is why Thomas says we "can reach out to the infinite" (1-2.2.8). We seek the infinite through the openness of desire, and only something indefectibly good will satisfy this desire.[3]

Thus charity establishes the possibility of a real relationship with God because charity directs infinite human desire to the Infinite

---

[3]Paul J. Wadell, C.P., *The Primacy of Love: An Introduction to the Ethics of Thomas Aquinas* (New York: Paulist Press, 1992), p. 61.

Good, which alone can satisfy that desire.

Moreover, the love of God made possible by charity flows outward into a love of other things: "We must assert that to love which is an act of the appetitive power, even in this state of life, tends to God first, and flows on from Him to other things, and in this sense charity loves God immediately, and other things through God" (2-2.27.4). As Aquinas explains, "God is the principal object of charity, while our neighbor is loved out of charity for God's sake" (2-2.23.5). The life of charity does not therefore involve a separation between the transcendent and the immanent but rather institutes a link between the two. The movement toward God that is constitutive of charity does not imply a movement away from the this-worldly but rather a more sufficient movement toward the goods of this world as well. In this way, charity overcomes the discontinuity between immanent and transcendent value which we noticed in Aristotle's account of human happiness.

Furthermore, as we love the things of this world out of charity, our activity transforms us into the love we seek to be. For Aquinas, it is not only that loving God rightly, we love all other things rightly; it is also that as we rightly love other things, these most ordinary activities transfigure our desires, making us ever more open and submissive to the love with which God graces us.

Because charity makes this integration possible, it also constitutes a principle of order that is otherwise lacking among the moral virtues. Aquinas states straightforwardly that "no order is assigned to the other virtues" (2-2.26.1), and this is indeed a worry that has troubled modern commentators on the virtue ethics tradition. For Aquinas, however, charity remedies the lack of an ordering principle among the natural virtues. Charity achieves this because it informs and orders every other virtue. Without charity, for Aquinas, the virtues lack the specific kind of directedness that they require, but charity provides precisely this directedness by ordering the other virtues to a common end: "Charity is said to be the end of other virtues, because it directs all other virtues to its own end. And since a mother is one who conceives within herself and by another, charity is called the mother of the other virtues, because, by commanding them, it conceives the acts of the other virtues, by the desire of the last end (2-2.23.8)."

Aquinas provides several examples of the way in which charity orders the other virtues. We are told that "the aspect under which our neighbor is to be loved, is God, since what we ought to love in our neighbor is that he may be in God" (2-2.25.1) and that "we can love irrational creatures out of charity, if we regard them as the good things that we desire for others, in so far, to wit, as we wish for their preservation, to God's honor and man's use" (2-2.25.3). Charity causes us to love our neighbor, ourselves, our enemies, our bodies and irrational creatures rightly, by ordering all of those loves to a more fundamental love of God (2-2.25).

Importantly charity does not operate as some abstract principle by the application of which we speculate about the right ordering of the life of practical virtue. Rather the supernatural virtue of charity comes with this ordering implicit, as it were. As we increase in charity and our love of God becomes more intense, Aquinas claims, the right ordering of all other loves follows naturally. Charity thus profoundly simplifies the moral life, not by making the practice of moral virtue irrelevant to the life of *eudaimonia*, but rather by habituating us to rightly order those practices as well as to rightly determine the significance of the finite goods of this life.

ADDICTION AND CHARITY

I am by no means the first to suggest a connection between addiction and humanity's quest for the transcendent. The eminent Swiss psychologist Carl Jung, who played a significant though unintentional role in the formation of Alcoholics Anonymous,[4] judged

---

[4]It was reported to Bill Wilson that Jung had told one of his alcoholic patients that there was for him, as for other chronic alcoholics, no hope of recovery excepting the rare possibility that he

that addictive "craving for alcohol was the equivalent, on a low level, of the spiritual thirst of our being for wholeness; expressed in medieval language: the union with God."[5] Jung found it significant that the Latin term for "alcohol" is *spiritus:* "You use the same word for the highest religious experience as well as for the most depraving poison. The helpful formula [for recovery] therefore is: *spiritus contra spiritum* (spirit against spirit)."[6] We might attempt to expand Jung's pregnant though cryptic claim by displaying the similarities between the theological habit of charity and the habit of addiction.

Aquinas says that charity orders the moral life because it is the form of every virtue. He says that "charity is called the form of the other virtues not as being their exemplar or their essential form, but rather by way of efficient cause" (2-2.23.8). How might one virtue be the efficient cause of another? Aquinas offers the following colorful scenario to display how one virtue can be the cause of another: "If one man commits adultery for the sake of gain and makes money by it, while another does so at the bidding of appetite though he loses money and is penalized for it, the latter would be held to be self-indulgent rather than grasping, but the former is unjust, but not self-indulgent" (1-2.18.6). To clarify: In the case of the man who commits adultery for the sake of gain, the vice of avarice causes the vice of lust to elicit the action of adultery. In the case of the man who squanders money in the pursuit of an adulterous relationship, the

---

"become the subject of a spiritual or religious experience—in short, a genuine conversion." In a letter to Jung, which can be found along with Jung's response in *The Language of the Heart: Bill W.'s Grapevine Writings* (New York: The A.A. Grapevine, 1988), pp. 276-81, Bill Wilson claims that it was the severity of this counsel that prodded him toward his own conversion and the eventual formulation of the first step of Alcoholics Anonymous. The two "grandfathers" of A.A. are therefore Carl Jung and William James, whose *The Varieties of Religious Experience* (New York: Mentor, 1958) was the other source of A.A.'s central tenet that recovery from alcoholism usually requires some kind of "conversion experience." See Susan Cheever, *My Name Is Bill* (New York: Simon & Schuster, 2004), for an account of the roles of Jung and James in the creation of A.A.

[5]Quoted in Francis Seeburger, *Addiction and Responsibility: An Inquiry into the Addictive Mind* (New York: Crossroad, 1993), p. 105.

[6]Ibid.

vice of lust commands the vice of prodigality to elicit the action of financial carelessness.

In like fashion, charity commands the other virtues to act as being directed to the end that charity seeks. Charity commands acts of justice, temperance, courage and so on *for the sake of* the realization of charity's end, friendship with God. In this way charity orders all virtue. It supplies the specific directedness toward a unified substantial end, which the virtues otherwise lack because they are at best directed to an abstract end (happiness or *eudaimonia*), which is always open to alternative specifications.

Addictions exert enormous control over human persons in part because they supply this need for an ordering principle. Like Aquinas's charity, addiction is a habit that commands all other activities of a person and directs each of those activities to a unified and substantial end. The person in the grips of major addiction finds that she operates in a profoundly simplified moral terrain, in which every activity, every relationship, every object of value is reinterpreted and invested with meaning only as it relates to the end of the practice of the addiction. Listen, for example, to the following testimonies:

> It was frightening that drink was being substituted for more and more of the things I really enjoyed doing. Golf, hunting, fishing were now merely excuses to drink excessively. . . . Never having enough, always craving more, the obsession for alcohol gradually began to dominate all my activities, particularly while traveling. Drink planning became more important than other plans. (AA 349)

> I had entered the drinking life. Drinking was part of being a man. Drinking was an integral part of sexuality, easing entrance to its dark and mysterious treasure chambers. Drinking was the sacramental binder of friendships. Drinking was the reward for work, fuel for celebration, the consolation for death or defeat.[7]

> Even today I vividly remember what it was like to organize my whole

---

[7] Pete Hammill, *A Drinking Life: A Memoir* (Boston: Little, Brown, 1994), pp. 146-47.

life around smoking. When things went well, I reached for a cigarette. When things went badly, I did the same. I smoked before breakfast, after a meal, when I had a drink, before doing something difficult, and after doing something difficult. I always had an excuse for smoking. Smoking became a ritual that served to highlight salient aspects of experience and to impose structure on what would otherwise have been a confusing morass of events. Smoking provided the commas, semicolons, question marks, exclamation marks, and full stops of experience. It helped me to achieve a feeling of mastery, a feeling that I was in charge of events rather than submitting to them. This craving for cigarettes amounts to a desire for order and control, not for nicotine.[8]

As each of these testimonies displays, addiction simplifies and orders life by narrowing the focus of the addicted person onto one object, one "final end." This phenomenon is sometimes overlooked because of the contemporary definition of addiction in terms of "loss of control." But what each of these testimonies makes plain is that the lure of addiction lies precisely in its ability to give the addicted person a sense of being in control of her life and of being able to assess and evaluate every possible course of action in terms of one definite end that eclipses every other contender for absolute allegiance.

Paradoxically the addicted person loses control over her addiction exactly to the extent that the ordering and controlling power of addiction insinuates itself into her view of the world. This is one source of the deep ambivalence characteristic of major addiction. Through rational deliberation and persuasion, the agent may come to believe that addiction has destroyed her life by wresting control away from her. But the habituated mind is not easily convinced, for it is precisely because of its ordering and controlling power that the object of desire has become an addicting object. When William Burroughs

---

[8]Jon Elster, *Strong Feelings: Emotion, Addiction, and Human Behavior* (Cambridge, Mass.: MIT Press, 1999), p. 64.

describes the life of the heroin addict as being "measured out in eye-droppers of morphine solution,"[9] we are likely to recoil in disgust. We fail to recognize, however, that the strength of the addiction resides, not primarily in the heroin or in the sensory pleasures that it provides, but rather in the simplicity and beauty of having one's life measured by one standard, harmonized with one melody, directed to one end.

Addictive objects are addictive because they enable persons to regulate their lives. This is why, among the various classes of mind-altering substances, very few persons are addicted to hallucinogens like LSD or mescaline. Hallucinogens are unpredictable in their effects such that the user can never know what type of "trip" to expect. Because hallucinogens cannot provide a regular experience, they cannot regulate the rest of experience. They lack the sameness and singularity of experience in light of which an addicted person might come to understand and interpret the worth of the rest of her activity. It is because hallucinogens cannot provide the "artificial sameness," which according to Stanton Peele "is the keynote of addictive experience," that they so rarely trigger the ordering habit of addiction.[10]

Understanding the ordering and regulating power of addiction puts us in a position to understand the sorts of lame "excuses" that alcoholics and other persons with addictions find for engaging in addictive behavior. The literature of Alcoholics Anonymous repeatedly reminds recovering alcoholics of this danger: "We had made the invention of alibis a fine art. We had to drink because times were hard or times were good. We had to drink because at home we were smothered with love or got none at all. We had to drink because at work we were great successes or dismal failures. We had to drink because our nation had won a war or lost a peace. And so it went, ad infinitum" (TT 47).

If *anything* can count as an excuse to use, then nothing seems like

---

[9]William Burroughs, *Junky* (New York: Penguin Books, 1977), p. xvi.
[10]Stanton Peele and Archie Brodsky, *Love and Addiction* (New York: Signet, 1975), p. 52.

a legitimate one. But there is more going on here than the mere invention of alibis. The fact that anything can count as an excuse to use is a function of the power that addiction has to incorporate every aspect of an addicted person's life into its own rhythms and rationales. It really *is* the case for the alcoholic that the good times are vacuous without alcohol, that the hard times are unbearable without alcohol, that loneliness doesn't feel lonely with alcohol, that loving relationships are mediated by alcohol, that success can only be celebrated with alcohol, that only alcohol can insulate from rejection and so on. To be an alcoholic is to enter into such a relationship with alcohol that everything else in life makes sense only if it is accompanied by alcohol. Like Aquinas's charity, addiction transfigures the most ordinary activities into meaningful transactions.

Aristotle claims that the practice of *theoria* is the best of all human activities because, among other reasons, "it is the most continuous, since we can contemplate truth more continuously than we can *do* anything" (1177a22-24). But even if it is the most continuous form of activity for Aristotle, it is nevertheless not altogether continuous. It is disrupted by our having to "do" things. Charity resolves this disruption. When infused with charity, the "doings" of an agent are not merely instrumental to some separate activity of charity but rather are partly constitutive of charity in that doing things out of charity is both an expression of and a growth in the agent's friendship with God. Even though Aristotle praises *theoria* as the "most continuous" activity available to human beings, he would have found it odd and irresponsible to advise anyone to "contemplate continually," for even the most virtuous person has to survive, and the things required for survival cannot count as contemplation. But given that practical activities can be performed in charity, Aquinas does not find it odd or irresponsible when Paul advises the faithful to "pray without ceasing" (1 Thess 5:17).

If the informing nature of charity makes possible Paul's otherwise impossible admonition to "pray continually," the informing nature of addiction makes possible what alcoholics call "thinking drinking"— the amazing capacity of the alcoholic to orient all of his or her thoughts and activities around the governing center of addiction.

> My friend Gail, who's a professional chef, used to get up at five A.M. and stand in her shower obsessing about what she'd drink that night, and when she'd be able to drink, and how and how much and with whom. She did this daily, obsessing in the shower about booze every morning at five A.M.[11]

> I had lived my entire life under the influence of mood and mind-altering substances. It wasn't that I was high on drugs every minute of the day—I was sometimes clean for several days at a time—but my obsession with drugs altered my perspective and my feelings about everything else, including my love for Mary, my relationship with my parents and siblings, my job, my soul, even my God. I hadn't just become addicted—addiction had become *me*.[12]

Addiction exploits "the instinctual need for one-pointedness; it distils the complexity of human experience into something essentially simple; it channels all needs into one."[13] This is the mark of addiction sometimes called obsession, but obsession does not, like Aristotle's *theoria*, exclude all other objects or activities from an agent's consciousness. Rather, obsession, like *caritas*, transfigures all other objects or activities in its own image and appropriates them for its own ends.

We turn finally to one more striking analogy between charity and addiction. Aquinas contends that charity is conditioned on the infinitude of human desire. Because "rational concupiscence is infinite," only charity, communion with the Infinite, can satisfy our hunger for wholeness: "We seek something so lovely that in possess-

---

[11]Caroline Knapp, *Drinking: A Love Story* (New York: Dial Press, 1996), p. 141.

[12]William Cope Moyers with Katherine Ketcham, *Broken: My Story of Addiction and Redemption* (New York: Viking, 2006), p. 140.

[13]William Pryor, *Survival of the Coolest: An Addiction Memoir* (Bath, U.K.: Clear Press, 2003), p. 132.

ing it we want no more," as Paul Wadell puts it.[14] Charity is able to provide this satisfaction because it offers a good that exceeds the natural human capacity for happiness. In what way is addiction a quest for this completion and, furthermore, an expression of the conviction that such completion lies, in a very real sense, beyond our natural human limitations?

We have already noted Jung's opinion on this matter; he believed that addiction was in fact a function of "the spiritual thirst of our being for wholeness; expressed in medieval language: the union with God." One could quote addicts at length on this point:

> Most alcoholics I know experience that hunger long before they pick up the first drink, that yearning for *something*, something outside the self that will provide relief and solace and well being.[15]

> Before A.A. we were trying to drink God out of a bottle.[16]

> [Addictive desires] have more to do with the soul than the brain. They illuminate the yearning for wholeness, for perfection, for making everything feel good and right again. They're about the deepest human hunger and thirst to experience rapture, joy, heaven.[17]

To put these testimonies in Aquinas's terms, addicted persons are persons who seem unable to deny that "rational concupiscence [desire] is infinite." The deep yearning for completion that is characteristic of addiction manifests itself in extremism, perfectionism and pursuit of ecstatic fulfillment, each of which parallels closely with features of charity.

Aquinas contends that unlike our other appetites—appetites for food, sex, wealth and so on—our appetite for God need not, indeed should not, be subjected to any moderation. Temperance is to love the sensory pleasures of taste and touch with moderation. Justice is

---

[14]Wadell, *Primacy of Love*, p. 39.
[15]Knapp, *Drinking*, p. 55.
[16]Bill Wilson, quoted in James Nelson, *Thirst: God and the Alcoholic Experience* (Louisville: Westminster John Knox Press, 2004), p. 27.
[17]Moyers, *Broken*, p. 207.

to love the good for another with moderation. Courage is to love the goods of life and honor with moderation. But charity is to love God without moderation. In fact, the measureless love of God that is charity, since it rightly orders all other acts to its own end, has the quality of imposing measure on every other habit. If we love God without limit, Aquinas thinks, we will find that we love every other good proportionately. Charity, therefore, directs us toward an object that we are to pursue without restraint, and charity promises us that extremism in this one direction will translate into right action in every other direction.

Addiction is, by definition, a habit of extremism: "Enough? That's a foreign word to an alcoholic, absolutely unknown. There is never enough, no such thing. . . . More is always better to an alcoholic; more is necessary. Why have two drinks if you can have three? Three if you can have four? Why stop?"[18] There is no such thing as the addictive "mean" or "moderate addiction."

Is the extremism of addiction a function of some surpassing or exceeding quality of the end it pursues? What, exactly, are addicted persons seeking when they engage in addictive behavior? Part of the purpose of my argument has been to demonstrate that persons with addictions are in search of a kind of order and integrity that seems to elude them in their day-to-day lives, whether because of the arbitrariness and fragmentation of modern culture or because of some deeper, more transcendent longing. What seems clear is that the addictive search is a search for something beyond the quotidian, the mundane, the little pleasures of the workaday grind. Francis Seeburger argues, "An addict is a person who wants *more*. Not 'more of the same,' more of the daily round of gains and losses, of goods and services that suffice for most of us most of the time, but 'more' in the sense of something altogether different, something no longer measurable by such everyday standards—something 'more than all that.'"[19]

---

[18]Knapp, *Drinking*, p. 53.
[19]Seeburger, *Addiction and Responsibility*, p. 114.

We might say that addicts are persons who are unsatisfied with the good life that is countenanced by Aristotle and which is ultimately rejected by Aquinas as a merely proximate form of happiness. Addictive desire is not *for* any proximate good but rather *against* every merely proximate good and for a good that is beyond the proximate. Addicts seek a perfection of happiness, rather than an approximation or measure. Addicts are, as A.A. describes them, "all or nothing people" (TT 161). They seek comprehensive happiness, nothing less than perfect contentment. This is why abstinence seems to be the only really successful response to addiction.

Addicts are simply not interested in imagining a life in which they pursue their ends moderately, in which the goods of addictive behavior are watered down and interspersed with more mundane pleasures in an attempt to provide a manageable way of life: "To me, the idea that a budding alcoholic can learn to drink moderately sounds like a contradiction in terms. (I rarely, if ever, drank moderately, even at the beginning.) It also seems to ignore the more deeply rooted, compulsive pulls a drinker feels toward alcohol; these are needs that don't respond well to the concept of moderation."[20] Aquinas would say the same of our desire for God: this is not a need that responds well to moderation.

The addictive pursuit of a something "more than all that," a something *beyond* the limitations of the self, is ultimately a pursuit of ecstasy. I am using "ecstasy" here in its formal sense, denoting a "standing outside of oneself," an ec-stasis. Charity, and the theological virtues in general, are *ecstatic* virtues in that the agent who receives these habits is at one and the same time the subject *and* the object of the habit. Charity, for example, inheres in the soul of an agent, but the action that is made possible through the habit of charity is really a derivative action, one that derives from a more fundamental activity on the part of God. Charity is possible only so long as God con-

---

[20]Knapp, *Drinking*, p. 119.

tinues to pour forth his eternally self-sufficient love into the soul of
the one whom he has befriended. It is therefore a habit that one *suffers* fundamentally and *enacts* derivatively.

Charity is, therefore, the realization of ecstasy, the movement beyond the confines of the self to a reality that comprehends the self
but is not contained by the self. This is why Aquinas speaks of charity as a habit of "participation" (2-2.24.5). Whereas the moral virtues
entrench and solidify the agency of the one who *possesses* them, charity displaces the agency of the one in whom it is "poured forth" by
taking possession of the agent.

Addiction, like charity, is a habit of ecstasy. Bruce Wilshire contends that "addictions are acts of violence directed at our own
insignificance."[21] If Wilshire is right about this, then the designa-
tion "drug abuse" is a euphemism; rather, some form of "self abuse"
is operative. Although Wilshire argues that the way to move beyond
addiction is by coming to grips with our own significance, a different interpretation is possible. For it may be that we are, relatively
speaking, insignificant. And, further, we may *rightly* believe that the
contentment for which we yearn does indeed lie outside of ourselves,
only to be realized through some ecstatic movement. This was the
position of Augustine, and the way in which he expresses his view is
of particular interest to our inquiry. Augustine prays: "You stir man
to take pleasure in praising you, because you have made us for yourself, and our heart is restless until it rests in you. . . . Who will enable
me to find rest in you? Who will grant me that you come to my heart
and *intoxicate* it, so that I forget my evils and embrace my one and
only good, yourself?"[22]

Addiction, then, might be understood as the quest for this ecstatic
intoxication. The addicted person, recognizing her own insignificance and her own insufficiency to realize perfect happiness, seeks

---

[21]Bruce Wilshire, *Wild Hunger: The Primal Roots of Modern Addiction* (Lanham, Md.: Rowman
and Littlefield, 1998), p. 14.
[22]Augustine, *Confessions*, I.i (1), v (5), emphasis mine.

to be taken up into a consuming experience, longs to be the object rather than the subject of experience, craves to suffer happiness rather than produce it. There is, then, a striking parallel between the would-be saint and the addict. As Francis Seeburger claims, "The genuine opposite of the addict is not the saint, but the lukewarm, complacent, comfortably 'decent' person represented by the rich young man of the Gospel. . . . The alcoholic or other addict stands in the shadow of the saint. In contrast, those who have never been addicted only because they lack enough passion for it are not even in sainthood's vicinity."[23]

The pull of addiction is this pull toward ecstasy, the expression of a deep discontent with the life of "just so" happiness, and the pursuit of an all-consuming love. This may explain why so many who lack the desperation or courage to pursue ecstasy through major addiction are nevertheless so mesmerized by reading addiction memoirs. Witness the national fascination with James Frey's 2005 addiction memoir *A Million Little Pieces*, which after being elevated to the status of an Oprah Winfrey Book of the Month, was discovered to be fraudulent.[24] It is suggestive to ask why it could be so lucrative to write or even to fabricate an addiction memoir. I suggest that it has something to do with the fundamental human quest for an ecstatic access to perfect, transcendent fulfillment.

Addictions are addicting just to the extent that they tempt us with the promise of such a perfect happiness, and they are enslaving just to the extent that they mimic and give intimations of this perfection. The depth and power of addiction become more intelligible as we come to see addiction as a counterfeit of the virtue of charity. As such, addiction is appropriately described as a failure of worship, a potent expression of idolatry in which we pursue in the immanent plane that which can only be achieved in relationship with the transcendent God. The cunning and allure of addiction is in fact brought

---

[23]Seeburger, *Addiction and Responsibility*, pp. 108, 112.
[24]James Frey, *A Million Little Pieces* (New York: Anchor, 2005).

out just to the extent that we see how stunningly addiction enables addicted persons to achieve simulacra of the goods that right worship makes possible. Such a display demonstrates that addiction can most fittingly be characterized as an enactment of the striving of human persons to attain on their own the flourishing, integrity of self and ecstatic delight that is only to be received through right relationship with God.

ADDICTION AS A WAY OF LIFE

Before turning to the theme of recovery, I want to wrap up this chapter by tying together all of the threads of the argument I have been weaving. In *Twelve Steps and Twelve Traditions*, we read: "Our sponsors declared that we were the victims of a mental obsession so subtly powerful that no amount of human willpower could break it" (TT 22). I have tried to provide an account of the ways in which addiction subtly yet powerfully enlists the allegiance of rationality and thereby becomes a "mental obsession." And I believe that this account puts us in a position to understand the recalcitrance of addiction to "human willpower."

Whatever means it employs, addiction does not insinuate itself through rational deliberation. It is not as though the addicted person, when confronted by the choice whether or not to act on her addiction, determines through deliberation that, all things considered, acting on the addiction is in her best interest. Indeed the paradox of addictive action is that it so often is performed in the face of rational deliberation to the contrary. The behavior of the addicted person becomes baffling, frighteningly so, precisely because it seems disconnected from the control that agents exert through deliberation. This is why persons with addictions often speak of "watching themselves" pour another drink or take another hit. And this is why addiction is experienced as a kind of enslavement or bondage, as a depletion rather than an enhancement of agency.

Caroline Knapp describes her own deluded and failed attempt to subject her alcoholism to the searching rays of discursive thought: "Child of an analyst that I am, I'd add insight to the list of remedies [I tried]—and I did, all the way to rehab. Tease out the *reasons* you drink. . . . *Think* your way to mental health."[25] According to Knapp, this is a dead end. Interestingly, though, Knapp does not conclude from this failure of the discursive searchlight that addiction is without its reasons or that addiction is fundamentally irrational. On the contrary, she claims that addiction is the enactment of a certain knowledge: "Over time, over many, many drinks, that knowledge is incorporated, the lessons folded into the soul: Liquor eases, liquor soothes and protects, a psychic balm."[26] This knowledge seems unhelpfully vague, but Knapp insists that any attempt to move beyond this level and to describe some more particular knowledge that addiction enacts can only be dishonest: "There is no simple answer. Trying to describe the process of becoming an alcoholic is like trying to describe air. It's too big and mysterious and pervasive to be defined. Alcohol is everywhere in your life, omnipresent, and you're both aware and unaware of it almost all the time; all you know is you'd die without it, and there is no simple reason why this happens, no single moment, no physiological event that pushes a heavy drinker across a concrete line into alcoholism. It's a slow, gradual, insidious *becoming*."[27]

The condition of being both "aware and unaware of [the object of addiction] almost all the time" sounds at first like an admission of self-deception or denial. Knapp speaks candidly about denial, and we shall have something more to say about the centrality of self-deception to addiction, but self-deception is not the only way to interpret this phenomenon of being simultaneously aware and unaware. We might also interpret it in terms of the difference between consciousness at the level of deliberation versus consciousness at the

[25]Knapp, *Drinking*, p. 117.
[26]Ibid., p. 59.
[27]Ibid., p. 9.

level of habit. We have already described how addiction, as it entrenches itself in the cogitative estimation of a person, takes on an ordering function in the addicted person's life, such that every other activity and good is rendered in terms of the calculus of addiction. But rarely is this ordering function spelled out at the level of explicit consciousness. Addiction may play this informing role without entering in as a term of syllogistic reasoning, without that is, factoring into an agent's deliberative consciousness.

In a remarkably insightful chapter titled *"In Vodka Veritas,"* Knapp tries to convey the way in which alcohol can become a mental obsession so subtle that we don't notice its becoming:

It's the equation we all lived by, every single alcoholic I know. . . .

Discomfort + Drink = No Discomfort
Fear + Drink = Bravery
Repression + Drink = Openness
Pain + Drink = Self-Obliteration[28]

This is "the mathematics of self-transformation." Knapp explains, "At heart alcoholism feels like the accumulation of dozens of such connections, dozens of tiny fears and hungers and rages, dozens of experiences and memories that collect in the bottom of your soul, coalescing over many many drinks into a single liquid solution."[29]

We might add to the equations:

Fragmentation + Addiction = Identity
Arbitrariness + Addiction = Consuming Purpose
Boredom + Addiction = Stimulation
Vacuity + Addiction = Meaning
Finitude + Addiction = Ecstasy

These are the equations, the reasons, that habituate the cogitative estimation. It is not the "many, many drinks" so much as these con-

---

[28]Ibid., pp. 61-70. I have drawn from several parts of this chapter to assemble a concentrated version of the case that she makes in narrative prose.
[29]Ibid., pp. 61, 69.

nections made and equations solved over the course of many drinks that habituate the cogitative estimation. As one recovering alcoholic explained to me, "for the alcoholic, alcohol is a pedagogue."

For the normal drinker, a drink is a drink. For the alcoholic, a drink is a life. Addiction is not something that an addicted person *has*, like a cough or a fever or even a disease. Addiction is a way of life. It is the habit of seeing the world a certain way and of being in the world a certain way. It is a habituation of perception, passion and imagination: the way that an addicted person perceives, feels, imagines—all of this is mediated by the meaning that her addiction has taken on in the cogitative estimation. Addiction, like most habits, instills intelligence in the emotions and imagination. Every act, even the most menial act that an addicted person performs, carries within itself this intelligence, this far-reaching and fundamental rationality of addicted being-in-the-world: "The life of an addict constitutes a vocation";[30] addiction is a "whole philosophy of life" (TT 25).

Neurologically this means that addiction is not primarily about the relationship between those specific neurons to which addictive substances may attach, thereby mimicking or blocking other "natural" neurotransmitters. These chemical reactions account for the processes of tolerance and withdrawal, but as was shown in chapter one, tolerance and withdrawal are not constitutive of addiction. Neurologically addiction entails the interrelation and interdependence of vast systems of cells that have to do with comfort, confidence, identity, meaning, purpose—in short, the terms of all of those "equations" performed, corroborated and recorded by the addicted person's cogitative estimation.

> A person who becomes temporarily addicted to narcotic painkillers in the hospital may be able to withdraw from the drug more quickly and with much greater serenity than another person can withdraw from the loss of a job or a loved one. The first person's addiction,

---

[30]Peele and Brodsky, *Love and Addiction*, p. 58.

although chemically intense, involves perhaps only a few million cells directly. It has not had time to influence such larger systems of cells as those having to do with the meaning of life, self-image, and basic security. . . . It is not so difficult to understand how our addictions can come to rule our lives. Each of our major addictions consists not only of the primary attachment itself; it also includes the involvement of multiple other systems that have been affected by it. To put it quite simply, addictions are never single problems. As soon as we try to break a real addiction, we discover that in many respects *it has become a way of life*.[31]

The subtlety and the power of addiction now come into focus as twin aspects of its nature as a complex habit substantially in the cogitative estimation but implicating the imagination and memory, as well as the body. It is subtle because it pervades every aspect of the addicted person's being such that she cannot step away from it, as it were, to locate it in one chain of reasoning or in one facet of consciousness. And it is powerful because whenever the addicted person attempts to rationally defeat her attraction to the addictive object, the object elicits a world of meaning, a whole inchoate and inarticulate "philosophy of life" that overflows and eludes straightforward practical reasoning. It is the nature of habit in general to be recalcitrant, to a greater or lesser degree, to the immediate and fleeting deliverances of deliberative reason, but this is especially true of habits of the cogitative estimation. For habits of the cogitative estimation generally operate as automatism habits, and thus they can operate quite independently of the conscious mental efforts of an agent—often in spite of those efforts.

Addiction, now entrenched as an automatism habit of the cogitative estimation, incorporates the object of addiction into a way of life so pervasively and seamlessly that the very effort to excise it often merely confirms and strengthens it. The first step of A.A.—"we

---

[31]May, *Addiction and Grace*, pp. 84-85, emphasis mine.

admitted we were powerless over alcohol"—is an acknowledgment of this paradox of addicted agency. The alcoholic in recovery must come to recognize that, precisely in attempting to exert control over her addiction, she solidifies and entrenches the addiction. The harder she tries to will straightforwardly not to drink, the more certain becomes her failure because, in focusing on the object of addiction, she incites a watertight world of meaning that can only be entered through the practice of the addiction.

One of the great insights of A.A. and of the twelve-step recovery model in general is the recognition of the addictive habit's recalcitrance to direct deliberation and willpower. It is for this reason, for example, that only one of the twelve steps—the first—even mentions alcohol. The other eleven steps can be understood as exhortations to address the problem, not by tackling it straight on, but rather by adopting alternative patterns of thought and action that may gradually reeducate and reform the habituated mind. The wisdom of the twelve-step program lies in the recognition that the habit of addiction can only be supplanted through the development of another habit that is as pervasive and compelling as the habit of addiction. One way of life can only be supplanted by another, and for this reason A.A. is rightly understood by its members to be a way of life: "The program is a plan for a lifetime of daily living" (AA 317).

Working the steps is not some magic formula that prevents the alcoholic from drinking while leaving him otherwise the same. The drug Antabuse (Disulfuram), which disposes the alcoholic to intense dysphoric experiences when combined with alcohol, is one attempt to provide such a magic formula, which is why it usually fails to accomplish lasting recovery. Rather, working the steps is about becoming the kind of person who does not perceive the world as an addict. This is at the heart of the A.A. adage that the fellowship is not mainly about teaching you how to quit drinking but about teaching you how to live sober. The addicted person who thinks of the steps as a temporary means to "get clean" will almost inevitably relapse. Becoming the kind of person who can work the steps as a way of life must be for the person in recovery an end in itself. The method is one of indirection. The addicted person takes on responsibility for aspects of her life that may be under more immediate control, that may not trigger the automatism habit of addiction, and in so doing, finds that she has indirectly responded to the addiction.

I have been investigating addiction without first offering a definition of it. I have not tried to carefully circumscribe the domain of addiction or to say what could and could not count as an addiction. Can a person be addicted to caffeine, shopping, exercise, a cause, a religion? Rather than delimit the boundaries of addiction, I have tried to focus instead on its center and to argue that addiction is a habit of the cogitative estimation according to which the object of addiction is invested with meaning that extends to every other aspect of an addicted person's life. I have argued that addiction is a habit that, like charity, informs all other habits by determining the end toward which those habits are directed. I have sometimes spoken of "major addiction" as a way of picking out this totalizing and pervading feature of the habit of addiction. I think it rare, for example, that coffee is the object of a major addiction. If we speak of an addiction to coffee, we tend to be focusing on tolerance and withdrawal as constitutive of addiction. As suggested in chapter one, such a narrow focus distracts us from those aspects of addiction that give alcoholism or crack-cocaine addiction, for example, their frightening and baffling power and allure. It is also possible, of course, for addictions to manifest some of the characteristics I have focused on and not others. For instance, I am convinced that smoking plays an important ordering and integrating role in the life of the smoker, but I am not sure how much nicotine addiction has to do with ecstatic desire.[32] I have tried to get at the center of what I take to be the most extreme and dominating addictions we know of—those in which

---

[32]However, an argument for a connection between smoking and the transcendent is made in Richard Klein, *Cigarettes Are Sublime* (Durham, N.C.: Duke University Press, 1993).

"loss of control" seems the only way to describe the addictive behavior—in the hope that other less severe addictions can nevertheless be illuminated by the investigation.

Although my own focus may call into question the status of certain addiction attributions such as caffeine addiction, in general the consequence of this focus will be a widening rather than narrowing of the domain of addiction. For there is no reason to suppose that substances are the only objects of desire that could play a totalizing role in an agent's life. Substance addictions rightly receive the attention that they do because of their visibly tragic effects, both on the lives of addicted persons and on the lives of those who care about them. But in some ways substance addictions are the less insidious kinds of major addictions precisely because they grow harder and harder to ignore. Other major addictions enslave quietly but are no less destructive of the humanity of those taken hostage.

My argument has been that addiction is a habit informed, as all habits are, by rationality, and I have been trying to probe the structure of this rationality. I have been trying to display how addiction insinuates itself into the cogitative estimation by supplying an order and integrity to an addicted person's life—order and integrity that we as human beings, and particularly as modern human beings, crave. Addiction, I have argued, operates as a moral and spiritual strategy, carrying out particular functions in the moral life and empowering a person for the pursuit, albeit misguided, of ecstatic satisfaction. This is why I have paid much attention to the constructive and positive potential of addiction and have elaborated little on the destruction and havoc it wreaks. Addiction is mysteriously powerful, but if we fail to ask what that power consists in, then we make it not only mysterious but also foreign. I have attempted to make addiction seem less foreign, giving us ways to think about the pull that addiction has on all of our lives. I hope my analysis has shown how near, rather than how far, each of us is to the major addict.

8

ADDICTION AND
THE CHURCH

THE GOSPEL AND THE HOPE OF RECOVERY

◆

If the analysis of addiction as a moral and spiritual strategy has been correct, what are the implications for the hope of recovery? More specifically, if as I have argued, the depth-dimension of addictive experience can only be brought out by understanding addiction as a counterfeit form of worship, what are the implications for the church? If addiction is false worship, how should the church, which hopes to practice true worship of the true God, respond to addiction?

This is not a "how to" chapter; I am not going to make specific recommendations about meeting formats or small group exercises or outreach programs that will help the church better respond to addicted persons in her midst. These sorts of recommendations are worthwhile, but they are not my concern here. Rather I am interested in thinking about what special challenges and opportunities addiction presents to the church. Addiction represents both a warning and an invitation to the church. The church has much to learn from those intentional communities in which recovery is happening. In many respects the prevalence of such communities can be seen as an indictment of the church. On the other hand, the church has resources for critiquing and deepening the recovery movement. In this concluding chapter I pursue three main lines of questioning. First, what distinguishes the church's worship from addiction? Second, what does the church have to offer to the recovery movement? And, third, what specific kinds of challenges and opportunities does addiction present to the church?

ADDICTION AND WORSHIP

Given the analysis of addiction that I have pursued, the most fundamental question that addiction raises for the church is whether worship is itself a form of addiction. Worship is adoration of, devotion to and complete submission to God. Right worship strives to relate all human desire and activity to God; it is an exercise in reorientation toward one all-sufficient end. All human desires and activities are put into question: How does this love, this commitment, this activity avow or disavow, affirm or disclaim my relationship to God as the fundamental expression of my identity and destiny? Worship is therefore a totalizing activity; it demands that *everything* in a person's life be put in the dock before God, interrogated by one standard and consequently renounced or reordered. This is why the form of worship is prayer. In confession we repent of that in us that does not conduce to love of God, and in praise and intercession we reorder our vision and our desires to the love of God. The end of right worship is that *everything* be taken captive for Christ, that our lives as Christians be the expression of one unceasing prayer to God.

How, then, is worship itself not simply another mode of addiction? After all, I have argued that addiction is characterized by a totalizing obsession with the object of addiction which, through the habituation of the cogitative estimation, pervades absolutely every aspect of an addicted person's life. If we take obsession as a constitutive mark of addiction, then we would be led to the conclusion that the nonaddictive life is the life that is obsession free, a life of neutrality or detachment. This is the conclusion that has been drawn in a large segment of the recovery movement. Francis Seeburger, for instance, argues that "the nonaddictive mind is a detached mind," and "the nonaddictive mind is an abandoned mind."[1] Buddhist or other Eastern religions are frequently lauded and recommended to addicted persons as conducive to the life of detachment.

If we accept the claim that the nonaddictive mind is the detached mind, and its converse, that the attached, dependent or obsessed mind is the addictive mind, then it becomes hard to imagine how worship, defined as complete adoration of, devotion to and submission to God, can be anything but another form of addiction. This has indeed been a common critique of religion that has emerged from the growing tendency to interpret all of human experience through the lens of the addiction paradigm. The critique is the source of the recurrent platitude heard among countless recovering addicts: "I'm spiritual, not religious." And the critique has led Christians to say bizarre things about the nature of their religious commitment. Thus, for example, William Lenters claims, "God wants us to be free from a dependent relationship with him."[2]

This is surely an unacceptable claim within the Christian grammar. Indeed Christian discipleship is nothing but a sustained exercise in learning how to reacknowledge our utter dependence on God, and sin is nothing if not the continued illusion that we can live independently of God. Lenters and others have been taken in by the identification of addiction with dependence, such that it seems that the only way to rescue Christian faith from the charge of addiction is by showing how, even within the Christian faith, we may maintain a kind of detachment and independence from the object of our devotion. However, our utter dependence on God and our obligation to live in submission to God are central Christian

---

[1]Francis Seeburger, *Addiction and Responsibility: An Inquiry into the Addictive Mind* (New York: Crossroad, 1993), p. 173.
[2]William Lenters, *The Freedom We Crave: Addiction: The Human Condition* (Grand Rapids: Eerdmans, 1985), p. 82.

convictions. Thus, within the Christian worldview, if addiction is conflated with dependence, there is no way to avoid the charge that devotion to God is an addiction. For how can the life of charity appear as anything but another form of addiction since it promises not detachment, but on the contrary, ecstatic participation in the consuming fire of the divine love. If, as Paul Wadell claims, "to love God in charity means we lose control over our life precisely where the risk is greatest: we lose control over our self,"[3] how is the saint really different from the addict who loses control over his life by submitting to the object of his addiction? How is worship really different from addiction?

Self-deception names one crucial difference between the addict and the saint and therefore between addiction and worship. We have explored most of the major "marks" of addiction—tolerance, withdrawal, craving, loss of control, ambivalence, relapse, obsession—with one significant exception. We have said very little about denial, that mark of addiction that is sometimes, like obsession, taken to be in and of itself a sufficient condition for addiction.[4] Although I do not believe either obsession or denial *alone* is a sufficient condition for addiction, taken together they are constitutive of the essence of addiction. Furthermore, the difference between addiction and worship can be spelled out in terms of denial.

Denial is a form, indeed the predominant form, of self-deception. Like incontinence, self-deception presents a paradox to philosophers intent on representing it in a noncontradictory way. In fact, the two paradoxes are intimately related, although the former has received the greater attention in the scholarly literature. Herbert Fingarette has written one of only two contemporary monographs on the subject, and his analysis provides a helpful point of departure for our

[3]Paul J. Wadell, C.P., *The Primacy of Love: An Introduction to the Ethics of Thomas Aquinas* (New York: Paulist Press, 1992), p. 91.
[4]"You often hear in A.A. meetings that denial *is* the disease of alcoholism, not just its primary symptom" (Caroline Knapp, *Drinking: A Love Story* [New York: Dial Press, 1996], p. 136).

own inquiry into the relationship between addiction and the self-deception that is denial.[5]

Fingarette proposes that self-deception should be understood not as the simultaneous maintenance of two mutually incompatible beliefs—which is indeed paradoxical if not outright contradictory—but rather as an agent's purposive avoidance of spelling out some feature of his engagement with the world when the agent is readily *able* to spell out that feature. There is nothing particularly paradoxical about this, but it does lead to a further question, one that Fingarette thinks is left out by standard accounts of self-deception as simultaneous maintenance of conflicting beliefs: Why would an agent intentionally and persistently avoid spelling out some feature of his engagement with the world?

Self-deception, according to Fingarette, is an exercise of identity formation. It is the response of an agent who finds himself engaged in the world in some way that he recognizes to be incompatible with the "person" or the "self" that the agent takes himself to be: "Self-deception turns upon the personal identity one accepts rather than the beliefs one has. . . . In general, the self-deceiver is engaged in the world in some way, and yet he refuses to identify himself as one who is so engaged; he refuses to avow the engagement as his."[6] Consciousness—the practice of spelling out who we are and what we are doing—is therefore a selective skill that is employed in the process of constituting an identity. And self-deception is part of this process whenever the formation of one's personal identity motivates the disavowal of certain of one's engagements in the world.

Contrary to our cherished intuitions, self-deception, rather than signaling a lack of character or integrity, is parasitic on the quest for integrity: "The less integrity, the less there is motive to enter into self-

---

[5]Herbert Fingarette, *Self-Deception* (London: Routledge, 1969). The other monograph on the subject is Alfred Mele's *Self-Deception Unmasked* (Princeton, N.J.: Princeton University Press, 2001).
[6]Fingarette, *Self-Deception,* p. 67.

deception. The greater the integrity of the person, and the more powerful the contrary inclination, the greater is the temptation to self-deception."[7] The married man who has long sought to be a faithful husband has powerful motives to deceive himself about what he is doing when he views pornography. The married man who could not care less about his integrity as a husband has no reason to self-deceive.

Generally, therefore, the problem of self-deception is not a function of moral laxity but, on the contrary, a manifestation of moral earnestness. One of the positive achievements of the propagation of the disease concept of addiction has been its ability to call into question the moral stigma attached to addiction. In doing so, the disease concept has helpfully counteracted the prevailing assumption that addiction is an extreme form of moral depravity. However, if we take addiction as a kind of habit group, and the skill or habit of denial as a constitutive habit of that habit group, we get a similar result: to the extent that addicted persons find reason to deceive themselves about their addictions, addiction cannot be characterized as moral depravity. It may represent a type of moral mistake or error, but addiction cannot be made intelligible as a kind of moral bankruptcy.

This insight allows us to make sense of a fact that is incomprehensible on the model of addiction as choice. For if addiction is merely a willful and morally depraved choice, then it would be astonishing that so many addicted persons could recover by practicing the Twelve Steps. If the defining characteristic of the addicted person is moral depravity, how could persons with addictions be expected to appreciate, let alone practice, the demands of honesty, humility and selflessness that are determinative of the twelve-step program of recovery? Paradoxically, to the extent that addicted persons are self-deceivers, they evidence a capacity for just this type of moral endeavor. Self-deception signals the presence of a genuine moral undertaking.

---

[7] Ibid., p. 140.

At the heart of addiction is a fundamental contradiction, and it is a contradiction that is ultimately its own undoing, holding out the hope of recovery. The enslaving force of addiction, I have argued, resides in its perverse promise to empower a moral agent to integrate and order his life around one all-consuming end. But addiction's promise is unmasked as a lie insofar as the agent comes to recognize that his addiction demands that he disavow projects and commitments that he knows must be included in a worthwhile life. Because it provides a simulacrum of the ordered and coherent life of flourishing, addiction ensnares. But the addict must come to disavow his addictive behavior precisely because addiction provides *merely* a simulacrum of what he knows to be his true end. Self-deception is the red flag here, signaling a discrepancy between what the addicted person had *hoped* addiction could provide and what addiction *does in fact* provide. Self-deception is the evidence that the totalizing devotion of addiction is a devastatingly deficient devotion. It cannot make good on its promise to incorporate those commitments that the agent knows must be incorporated into any life of genuine flourishing. Addiction achieves integrity and internal order only by demanding the rejection of certain goods—consistent family life, transparent friendships, productive work—that the addicted person is ultimately unwilling to disavow. In turn, the addiction, which has already through the power of its lie insinuated itself in the addicted person's cogitative estimation, must itself be disavowed. Denial, therefore, testifies simultaneously to the power of addiction's promise and the acknowledgment that the promise is a lie. This is the wisdom behind the A.A. adage: "You are only as sick as your secrets."[8]

Thus addiction is not merely any and every dominating and all-consuming purpose. Rather, addiction is any and every dominating and all-consuming purpose whose insufficiency to sustain the self in his or her pursuit of a worthwhile life is manifested in de-

---

[8]Moyers, *Broken*, p. 225.

nial. This is why addicted persons are notoriously poor at meditation and why A.A. so frequently recommends meditation as central to the life of recovery. Meditation forces us to reflect on the stories that we tell ourselves about our lives, and it therefore represents a very real threat to any addiction since it threatens to reveal the insufficiencies of those stories. To the extent that saints are exemplars in the practice of meditation, we have reason to doubt that worship is an addiction.

The theological challenge that addiction poses to the church is whether it can invite people into a life of devotion and dependence that is not self-deceptive. Addiction teaches us that devotion to one consuming end and dependence on one overriding good can lead, indeed usually does lead, to self-deception. For such devotion and dependence are almost always an attempt to bestow an order and integrity on our lives in such a way that we must ignore or deny the fundamental disorder and disunity of the self. Addictive devotion and dependence then become strategies of control, modes of fashioning a self and structuring an identity, which are fundamentally dishonest because we are not in control of our lives. Addiction is seductive because it promises to address the disorder and disunity of the self without requiring that we relinquish control over our own lives. In this sense, addiction performs the contradiction that is sin. Because we strive to live independently from God, our lives are disordered and fragmented; we attempt to resolve the disorder and fragmentation by a reassertion of our own independence; thus the order and unity that we achieve is always illusory and requires that we deceive ourselves about who we are.

Right worship, on the other hand, trains us to see that the disorder and disunity of the self are themselves a symptom of our sinful insistence on maintaining control over our own lives. Such disorder and disunity therefore cannot be rectified by anything that we might do but only by renouncing our claim to be able to establish an impermeable and unified identity. Worship trains us to see that the self is not something that we establish but rather something that we continually receive from God. As Stanley Hauerwas points out, "There has always been something right about the traditional understanding that the unity of the self and the knowledge of God are correlates. Such a unity does not come automatically. It is a slow achievement as we work day in and day out to locate ourselves within God's story. We inherently resist such a locating because we have come to love our sinfulness—and we fear losing it."[9]

The difference between addictive dependence and faithful dependence on God is therefore the difference between a dependence that is fundamentally an exercise of control and a dependence that is fundamentally an exercise of renunciation and relinquishment. It is the difference between the life of sin and the life of grace. In the language of habit, it is the difference between acquired and infused virtue. This is the theological insight that led Augustine to claim that acquired virtues are always at best "glittering vices" (*splendida peccata*); since they are "achieved" rather than "received" they serve to underwrite the sinful assumption that we may establish a coherent self apart from dependence on God. Whereas acquired virtues are produced by our own virtuous activity, infused virtues are produced in us by God. We are the "active principle" of acquired virtue; God is the "active principle" of infused virtue (1-2.62.1). And this is why Aquinas insists that in regeneration the believer receives not only the infused supernatural virtues of faith, hope and love, but also the infused moral virtues, which are distinct from the acquired moral virtues (1-2.63.3). The acquired moral virtues are developed through moral exertion and are directed toward the end of consolidating a self that can withstand the storms of time and fortune. By contrast, the infused moral virtues are received by grace and are directed toward the end of friendship with God.[10]

---

[9]Stanley Hauerwas, *The Peaceable Kingdom: A Primer in Christian Ethics* (Notre Dame, Ind.: Notre Dame University Press, 1983), p. 47.

[10]For a helpful discussion of Aquinas's theory of the infused moral virtues that considers those

Moreover, infused virtue is not a one-time gift, any more than acquired virtue is a one-time achievement. We may grow in the supernatural virtues of faith, hope and love because of the continuing work of the Spirit who indwells us. For Aquinas, God's gracious bestowal of faith, hope and love makes possible "a kind of participation of the Godhead, about which it is written (2 Pet. i. 4) that by Christ we are made *partakers of the Divine nature*" (1-2.62.1, emphasis in original). Thus Christian worship graciously displaces us from being the center of our story and instead incorporates us into the story of God. Worship of the triune God releases us from the need to justify ourselves through strategies of self-deception by continually revealing that we are justified by Christ alone. And worship of the triune God relieves us of the burden of achieving our own identity and sustaining our own story by drawing us, through the work of the Spirit, into the life of God.

THE CHURCH AND THE HOPE OF RECOVERY

Distinguishing the right worship of the church from the counterfeit worship of addiction places us in a position to explore ways in which the church should conceive of recovery from addiction. A helpful approach to this sort of question pushes us to ask about the relationship between the life of the church and the practice of recovery as it is understood and embodied within the most dominant recovery paradigm, that of the twelve-step recovery movement. The structure of A.A.'s twelve-step program has been adapted to respond to a wide variety of addictions, and this expansion has been so successful that the twelve-step program is now widely taken to be the definitive response to addiction of any kind.[11]

---

virtues particularly in relation to the acquired habit of alcoholism, see Michael S. Sherwin, O.P., "Infused Virtue and the Effects of Acquired Vice: A Test Case for the Thomistic Theory of Infused Cardinal Virtues," *The Thomist* 73 (2009): 29-52.

[11]For an attempt to assess the merits of the several distinct recovery philosophies, see Lonnie Shavelson, *Hooked: Five Addicts Challenge Our Misguided Drug Rehab System* (New York: New Press, 2001).

Generally the relationship between the church and the twelve-step movement has been positive. Many churches donate or lease space in their buildings for twelve-step meetings. Other churches have adopted and adapted the twelve-step movement in order to provide recovery opportunities for addicted persons within the church. Some of the adaptations are theologically careful; others are more haphazard, merely baptizing the twelve-step program without questioning the theological assumptions that are implicit in its basic set of principles and goals.[12]

Despite significant collaboration between the church and the twelve-step movement, many have claimed, I think rightly, that the massive growth of twelve-step groups has exposed the church's inability or failure to deal honestly and adequately with the brokenness of persons. We must ask, then, what it is that these movements provide that the church often fails to provide. However, beginning with this kind of question is dangerous because it presupposes that the church has the same mission as that of the twelve-step recovery movement. It is important, therefore, to begin by asking about ways in which the church's mission and the church's understanding of addiction and recovery might need to be distinguished from the mission and philosophy of the twelve-step movement. Only then should we move to ask about the ways in which the twelve-step movement can call the church back to a greater faithfulness to addicted persons.

The twelve-step recovery movement rightly recognizes that addiction is an exercise of self-assertion and control that leads the addicted person to deny his own underlying disorder and disunity. The twelve-step movement seeks to remedy this in two ways. First, the addicted person seeking recovery must acknowledge a power greater than himself on which he is dependent. Thus the third step teaches:

---

[12]An example of an adaptation of the twelve-step program that evidences an awareness of many of the theological issues at stake is the "Celebrate Recovery" program launched in 1995 by Saddleback Church in Lake Forest, California. See http://celebraterecovery.com.au/index .php.

"We made a decision to turn our will and our lives over to the care of God *as we understood him*" (TT 5, emphasis in original). Second, the addicted person seeking recovery must adopt as his most fundamental identity that of "alcoholic" or "addict." Thus every time that a person wishes to speak in a meeting of Alcoholics Anonymous or some similar twelve-step recovery program, he or she must begin with the introduction, "I'm Joe, I'm an alcoholic," or, "I'm Sue, I'm an addict."

The church must be circumspect about straightforwardly adopting the paradigm of the twelve-step recovery movement. For although these requirements are salutary and have been helpful to many addicted persons seeking recovery, from the perspective of the church's worship they do not go far enough, and they risk reinstituting the fundamental orientation that underlies addiction. In Christian worship we encounter God not as we understand him, but as he is revealed to us in the Scriptures and in the liturgy. Of course, our encounter with God is never unmediated, but in worship Christians have to do with a God who has a determinate character and has acted determinatively in history. We are not invited in worship to project a "God as we understand him," but rather to be encountered by the God of Israel and of Jesus Christ, whose particularity places not only our own "God-consciousness" but even our own sense of self into question. Thus the following invitation printed on a pamphlet of a well-known twelve-step treatment center can only seem perverse from the perspective of right Christian worship: "What you want to achieve is the gift of a blank slate, with a pencil poised in your own hand to redraw the image. . . . What do you need to draw a new image, your *own* image of a Higher Power? . . . What does a Higher Power need to do for you? . . . What form should that Higher Power take? What's best—most comfortable—for you?"[13]

The invitation to fashion a God who can meet our perceived needs

---

[13]Quoted in Linda Mercadante, *Victims and Sinners: Spiritual Roots of Addiction and Recovery* (Louisville: Westminster John Knox Press, 1996), p. 157.

is indeed an invitation to self-deception and therefore can only inhibit authentic recovery from addiction. In fact, it is precisely the human tendency—so devastatingly illuminated by Feuerbach—to make God in our own image that opens up "religion" to the critique that it is but another form of addiction. Karl Barth employed Feuerbach's analysis to draw a distinction between "religion," which is humanity's effort to commune with God on its own terms, and "faith," which is communion with God initiated and established by God's self-revelation. For Barth, "religion is the contradiction of revelation. That which pleases God is not human religiosity but faith in response to divine revelation; revelation that proceeds only and directly from the triune God."[14] Whereas many in the recovery movement style themselves "spiritual but not religious," Christian worship should train us to be neither "spiritual" nor "religious" but rather to be dependent on the triune God of Israel who became incarnate in Jesus of Nazareth. This is not a dependence that the Christian must achieve; as the language of infused virtue is meant to indicate, this is a dependence that we are free to receive. The Holy Spirit constantly woos us, offering to relieve us from our own self-absorption and "guide us into all the truth" (Jn 16:13).

Theologically, overconfidence in our own sense of self is a correlative of an indeterminate and equivocal view of God. It is a question of priority: if we are certain of our own identity and character, then the identity and character of God must be conditioned by this certainty. Alternatively, if we are certain of the identity and character of God, then our own sense of self is always conditioned by our relationship to God. This is the upshot of Hauerwas's claim that "the unity of the self and the knowledge of God are correlates." In this sense Christian identity is always *relative*. To say that we are sinners is not to stake out an identity but rather to name a relation. To acknowledge that we are sinners is to acknowledge that we lack

---

[14]Karl Barth, *Church Dogmatics* 1/2, ed. G. W. Bromiley and T. F. Torrance (London: T & T Clark, 1963), pp. 302-3.

the resources for knowing who we are apart from God.

Thus the correlative to the twelve-step movement's vague conception of God is overconfidence in the identity of "addict." Slogans like "once an alcoholic, always an alcoholic" (AA 33) are intended to humble the pride of the recovering addicted person and to dispel any illusion that the addiction is a mere appendage to the self, something that persons with addictions may put on or take off at will. Such slogans are valuable to the extent that they remind the addicted person that his addiction has become a part of himself, that it is intertwined with his character to such a degree that recovery necessitates a conversion of character. Yet, from the Christian perspective, such identity statements run the risk of rehearsing the illusion at the heart of all addiction, and indeed at the heart of all sin, namely the illusion that we can know who we are apart from our relationship to God. Ironically such identity statements may become a source of pride, such that persons recovering from addiction may feel belittled or discounted at the suggestion that "addict" is not necessarily who they are. "Alcoholic" or "addict" has then become part of a cherished identity, a core of the self that is not open to interrogation and is not conditioned by some more fundamental reality.

Additionally, the adoption of "alcoholic" or "addict" as one's identity inevitably places limitations on the scope of recovery. If my addiction is fundamental to who I am, if it is basic to my being, then the life of recovery can never be more than a daily denial of my true self. The literature of A.A. often talks this way: all that the alcoholic can hope for from the recovery process is "a daily reprieve" from drinking (AA 85). This view of recovery is tragic, for it insists that there is a primordial and ontological discomfiture between who one is and how one must behave. Such a tragic view, in rejecting the hope of a final harmony between being and act, contains an implicit "theology of creation," which is ultimately in conflict with a Christian understanding of creation. As Linda Mercadante has argued, "presenting the addictive vulnerability as integral to the person skates dangerously close to the Manichaean picture of human nature," according to which there is an ontological duality between good and evil such that the ultimate triumph of good over evil would require the total destruction of human nature.[15] Within this picture, the addicted person is consigned to a life of tragedy.

In contrast, the Christian view of recovery is a function of the Christian view of redemption, which is almost profligate and reckless in its hopefulness. For at the heart of the Christian view of redemption is the insistence that sin is not fundamental or ontological but rather historical and contingent. Therefore Christians live into the hope that their destiny is a harmony between who they are and what they want and do, between their being and their act. On this view our freedom is not ultimately at odds with our nature but is rather the fullest expression of our true nature. The process of discovering our true nature and therefore our complete freedom is the process of sanctification. As we are sanctified, we come to locate ourselves completely within God's story about who we are and what we most fundamentally desire.

The scope of recovery is therefore radically extended within a Christian view of addiction. Indeed "recovery" does not sufficiently name the Christian hope in the face of addiction. Instead the Christian hopes for "discovery" and "new creation"—not a return to some maintainable equilibrium between who we are and what we want but rather a transformation of the self that brings who we are and what we want (which are in tension only because of the contingent and proleptically vanquished power of sin) into perfect coordination and harmony.

Given my argument that addiction is a habit, it is the Christian view of recovery that is the more philosophically defensible. For habits, we must remember, are *qualifications* of the self and therefore must never be identified with the self. In claiming the identity of

---

[15]Mercadante, *Victims and Sinners*, p. 118.

"addict" or "alcoholic," we deny that addiction is a habit and assert instead that it is an entity. But on the Christian view, addiction is indeed a habit that may be transformed into charity. For these reasons, I have tended to speak of "addicted persons" and "persons with addiction" rather than to speak of "addicts."

I know from personal conversations that this line of argument is unwelcome to many within the recovery movement. It sounds too optimistic, insufficiently circumspect, like an invitation to hubris and reckless self-confidence. Yet within the Christian understanding such a hope is undeniable. To insist that our identities are ontologically and finally disordered is simply a denial of the Christian doctrine of salvation. If the church is to be faithful, it must therefore be unwavering in its commitment to a final liberation from the bondage of sin over both our act and our being. That is the Christian eschatological hope, and such a hope cannot but transform our understanding of addiction and recovery.

RECOVERY AND FRIENDSHIP

If the church has resources for offering an even deeper hope to recovering persons than that offered by the twelve-step movement, why has the twelve-step movement essentially replaced the church as the place that addicted persons go to recover? This is a difficult question, for the hope that is held out by the church is indeed good news, but to recognize it as such is already to be converted. The sinner within each of us is repelled by the invitation to relinquish any and every claim on our lives, and we therefore are inclined to seek out methods of amelioration that do not demand such a renunciation. Nevertheless, many addicted persons who are Christians maintain that they find within the embrace of the twelve-step recovery movement what they cannot find within their own churches. This is a serious indictment to the church, and we must ask where the church has failed in comparison to the twelve-step movement.

I am convinced that the twelve-step movement has been successful largely because of the way in which its format and method invite and demand transformative friendships. That deep friendships are in fact necessary to the life of recovery is widely acknowledged. The overwhelming majority of addicts testify to the power of friendship as the single most important factor in their recoveries from addiction.

> But the most compelling part of A.A., the part that made me want to try this sober thing, was the laughter, the pure joy of the laughter that I heard only from sober alcoholics. (AA 333)

> I found my tribe, the social architecture that fulfills my every need for camaraderie and conviviality. (AA 336)

> A.A. is my home now. . . . I no longer feel alone. (AA 346)

> The thing that kept me sober until I got a grip on honesty was the love in the room of Alcoholics Anonymous. I made some friends for the first time in my life. Real friends that cared, even when I was broke and feeling desperate. (AA 468)

Twelve-step recovery groups have become those places where addicts feel assured that they will find genuine fellowship. Why are twelve-step groups so successful at providing space for transformative friendships? I would like to suggest three ways in which they have been especially adept at the practice of friendship. In each of these ways the twelve-step movement serves to recall the church to a biblical understanding of friendship and fellowship.

First, whereas the twelve-step movement insists on treating its members as recovering addicts, the church does not always insist on treating its members as repentant sinners. I have argued that "sinner" is a much more radical attribution than "addict" because it challenges the addicted person's attempts to stake claim to an identity that is independent of God. In this way I think that the label "addict" is ultimately insufficient to name the depth of the disorder that is addiction. This is quite irrelevant, however, if persons within the church do not live as though they are repentant sinners.

The wisdom of A.A. is contained in its *celebration* of an addict's recognition and public acknowledgment that he is an addict. Such a recognition and acknowledgment is deemed an *achievement* and is celebrated by being ritualized and reiterated. Indeed, within the twelve-step movement, even the relapse of one of the members is received, rehearsed and discussed by the larger group as a gift since it serves as a concrete reminder that each member of the group is susceptible to the same fate. Moreover, the central activity of twelve-step fellowship meetings is the practice of narrating the lives of members within the paradigm of recovering addict. Coming to grips with this status is not in any sense peripheral to what the group does but is rather what the group is all about. Thus, when a member speaks of craving, withdrawal, depression, loneliness or even relapse, he is not raising an issue that must be dealt with before the group can move on to its business; he is doing the group's business. Such testimonies are the liturgy of the twelve-step movement. The group has been formed exactly to hear and respond to such testimonies.

The church has too often been less committed to fostering an atmosphere in which its members feel not only free but indeed expected to publicly recognize their status as sinners and to narrate their lives to others within this paradigm. Theologically the recognition of one's status as sinner is also an achievement, yet we often do not treat it as such. Obvious logistical challenges crop up here, yet I think these challenges can be overstated. Much more central to the church's failure to provide fellowship to the addicted persons in its midst is its failure to live out its biblical calling to train disciples to narrate their lives as repentant sinners: "If we say that we have no sin, we deceive ourselves, and the truth is not in us" (1 Jn 1:8). Biblically the mandate to truthfully and publicly declare our sinfulness is crucial to our growth in holiness: "*If we confess our sins*, he who is faithful and just will forgive us our sins and cleanse us from all unrighteousness" (1 Jn 1:9, my emphasis).

Of course, many of us are not sure we want to be in a church that so trains us, for that would entail not only our humiliation but also a vulnerability to others in which many of us have no interest. We are afraid that if we confessed our sins, other people might make claims on our lives by insisting on praying for us and asking us how we are doing. Most of us are not sure that we want church to be that involved.

I do not mean to sound cynical. Of course the church is full of people who wish for honest and vulnerable relationships and genuinely seek to be trained to faithfully narrate their lives as sinners. Nevertheless the church seems to be a place where this kind of investment is optional, and in this respect it differs profoundly from Alcoholics Anonymous and other twelve-step movements. For if one did not desire such vulnerability, accountability and interdependence, what would be the point of attending an A.A. meeting? Yet many of us think something is to be gained from the church apart from learning to acknowledge our sinfulness and our utter dependence on God. To the extent that the church legitimates this error—by offering, instead, social capital, childcare, entertainment, family time and so on—the church is accountable for its failure to provide hospitality, sustenance and redemption to the addicted persons in its midst.

Second, the twelve-step movement is skilled at friendship because it demands that its members enter into certain kinds of relationships that are structured toward a particular end. In this respect the twelve-step movement lives out the Aristotelian insight that one of the chief purposes of friendship is "training in virtue." Aristotle says that "a certain training in virtue arises also from the company of the good" (1170a11-13). We are not accustomed to think that training is part of friendship. Training is something that we do "on the job," and friendship is our escape from the tedium and paternalism implied by "training." But Aristotle thinks that one feature of certain types of friendships is that they will involve training.

We should not be surprised, for training is skill language, habit language, and indeed Aristotle thinks that certain friendships will be characterized by a sort of master/apprentice relationship. This insight, although somewhat foreign to popular conceptions of friendship, is familiar to those recovering in the twelve-step tradition. One of the more important pieces of advice offered to newcomers— *Twelve Steps and Twelve Traditions* instructively calls them "novices" (TT 60)—is that they find a "sponsor," usually someone who has "worked the steps" for a number of years and has developed habits of character that the novice can emulate and from which the sponsor can advise and encourage the novice. The philosophical assumption behind the sponsor/novice setup is ancient and deeply Aristotelian, but somewhat alien in our context where the moral life is most immediately associated with learning certain abstract rules or principles that we can apply to "dilemmas." The basic philosophical assumption embodied in the sponsor/novice relationship is that "it is easier to act yourself into a new way of thinking than to think yourself into a new way of acting" (AA 366). This is why it is rarely enough that one simply receive the advice and instruction offered at A.A. meetings and read from the Big Book. The recovering "apprentice" needs a "master," or several: "I learned how to be a good A.A. member by watching good A.A. members and doing what they do" (AA 521).

The church fails to provide sustaining and transforming relationships for addicted persons in its midst wherever and whenever it buys into the modern assumption that growth in virtue is a product of learning abstract principles whereas friendship is a private endeavor that is based on "similar interests." Such an assumption is in direct opposition to the biblical understanding of friendship. Although affection characterizes many of the friendships portrayed in the Bible, affection is ancillary to the animating center of friendship, which is nothing less than the willingness to lay down one's life for one's friend (Jn 15:13). Such friendships are not optional for Christians; Jesus *commands* his disciples to befriend one another in this distinctive way. Moreover, Paul recommends that new converts and those who are young in the faith should "devote themselves to the service of the saints" (1 Cor 16:15) and place themselves under "the authority of the elders" (1 Pet 5:5). For Paul, friendships of accountability and training are central to growth in holiness.

The church must be bold to implement relational structures that are explicitly designed for training in virtue. Thus mentoring programs in the church ought not to be something parishioners must seek out but rather something so prevalent that parishioners would have to intentionally avoid them. The twelve-step insight that recovery is primarily an exercise of friendship and only secondarily a consequence of hearing and reading from the Big Book applies to the church as well. In the absence of concrete, specified relationships of accountability, imitation and mutual prayer, the practice of the liturgy is of limited worth. It is true that the liturgy of the church is the work of the people, but it is a work that only makes sense in the context of relationships that embody, test and strive for the truth that the liturgy makes known.

Finally, and closely related to this second feature of friendship, the twelve-step movement rightly recognizes that transformative friendship requires physical proximity and the sharing of considerable amounts of time together. Here too the twelve-step movement capitalizes on an ancient Aristotelian insight about the nature of friendships conducive to virtue. Aristotle says, "There is nothing so characteristic of friends as living together" (1157b19-20). This too seems to be a bit overstated given our contemporary lifestyle. That our careers might physically separate us from our friends is taken to be a matter of fact and a relatively minor setback to friendship, which can be mitigated by the rapid advances in communication technology.

Would Aristotle have placed such emphasis on sharing common space and time with friends if he could have been "online"? I suspect that he would have, for Aristotle believed that physical proximity, actually sharing space-time with our friends, is essential to friendship not only because we delight in the company of our friends (which, after all, can still be enjoyed "long distance") but also because the practice of virtue demands it. Aristotle believed that character friendships require sharing life together because persons who are striving to live well need to be affirmed and confirmed in their conviction that the activities in which they are engaging are worthy of their time and energy. Paul Wadell puts it this way: "One cannot afford to tire of virtue because to become disengaged with its activities is to begin a deterioration of self no one can long endure. Friendship is especially crucial because without the support and reassurance of others who are involved with us in the virtuous life, we invariably grow disenchanted with the very activities we cannot afford to doubt."[16]

That members of A.A. actually meet in rooms and sit around tables and share coffee every or nearly every night of the week is not merely incidental to the recovery of its members. The importance of place and "dailyness" for the success of A.A. cannot be overstated. Many nonaddicts are surprised to hear from recovering addicts who have been sober for years that they still attend A.A. meetings four or five nights of the week. But that they do is essential, not only to their own sobriety, but particularly to the efforts of newcomers and "novices." When an A.A. member with his 10-year chip puts on his shoes, gets in his car, drives to the rented room or church basement, gets the coffee brewing, sits through the meeting quietly, stays after to talk with old friends and skeptical newcomers, locks up the room, gets in his car and drives home, none of the intentionality that accompanies each of those actions is lost. Every basic act testifies and sanctifies the worth of the shared endeavor.

If the church is to be a place where addicted persons may find redeeming fellowship, it will have to become a primary social hub. It must facilitate and expect of its members friendships that are rooted in the day-to-day sharing of ordinary activities. We tend to think of

---

[16]Paul J. Wadell, C.P., *Friendship and the Moral Life* (Notre Dame, Ind.: University of Notre Dame Press, 1989), pp. 59-60.

our "work friendships" in this way simply because we see the people we work with on a daily basis. But if the church is to provide a genuine alternative to addicted persons seeking recovery, it must provide daily, rather than once-weekly opportunities for communal worship, testimony and prayer, and it must challenge its parishioners to treat the church as their primary social community. Here, too, the twelve-step movement can recall the church to its biblical roots. For one of the distinctive marks of the vibrant early Christian community was its devotion to sharing space and time with one another in the activities of daily life: *"Day by day, as they spent much time together in the temple,* they broke bread from house to house and ate their food with glad and generous hearts, praising God and having the goodwill of all the people" (Acts 2:46-47, my emphasis).

ADDICTION AS PROPHETIC CHALLENGE

All sin is idolatry, and therefore all goods that are pursued as if they were gods are pursued sinfully. But much of the time our sinfulness is easily unmasked because the goods that we have elevated to an inordinate status so plainly fall short of our exalted expectations. They fail to supply the kind of control, integrity and ecstasy that we long to achieve. Such goods are not likely to be seriously mistaken for all-sufficient goods. They are, rather, distractions and diversions, ways of ignoring or repressing our deep restlessness.

Addiction is—like all sin—a form of idolatry because it elevates some proximate good to the status of ultimate good, a status that belongs to God alone. But addiction is uniquely alluring, uniquely captivating and uniquely powerful because its object comes so close to making good on its false promise to be God. All sin is an attempt to overreach our powers and to establish on our own a flourishing and fulfillment that can only be found within right relationship to God. In this sense all sin is rebellion against God. But addiction is powerful, captivating and alluring because it is a rebellion that comes so close to succeeding. Major addiction is not necessarily the most

tempting form of idolatry; it is too extreme, totalizing and demanding to tempt many of us. But exactly because it is so extreme, totalizing and demanding, addiction is the most potent form of idolatry
on offer.

Because addiction is the most potent form of idolatry available to
modern persons, it presents a particular challenge to the church. In
important respects addiction is unlike the response to anxiety and
restlessness that takes the more "respectable" forms of diversion and
distraction such as shopping, entertainment or hobbies. Unlike these
latter kinds of response, addiction does in its own perverse way enable an agent to confer shape and meaning on his existence since it
brings with it its own impetus, ordering end, integrative energy and
world of meanings. Because of this, the life of distraction and diversion would, in a very real, sense constitute a loss of meaning for the
addicted person, and it is therefore unlikely that such a life could
provide a rationale as compelling as the rationale of addiction.

This is, I suspect, why many of us in the church feel so powerless
in the face of addiction. We feel the power of addiction in our own
lives, and we doubt that the gospel is strong enough to overcome it.
Of course, we do not say this sort of thing. We are even committed
by our beliefs to denying it. But when an alcoholic stumbles into
church, when we learn that our pastor has been addicted to pornography for the past ten years, when we drive through the local ghettos
and slums that are decimated by addiction, the immediate response
for many of us who call ourselves Christians is despair. Is the gospel
really powerful enough for all this?

I suspect that many of us feel this way because we doubt the power
of the gospel over our own lives. We wonder if we have escaped the
grip of addiction, not because of the power of the gospel, but because
of circumstances, temperament, fear of rejection or cowardice. Perhaps, unlike the addict, we have not demanded an all-consuming
purpose, a coherent and integrated life, and an ecstatic participation
in some all-sufficient and transcendent good. For so long we have

told ourselves that, in the words of the Rolling Stones, "you can't always get what you want," and we have used this justification to dull and suppress our deepest longings for rest, peace and joy. We have settled instead for a life of respectability, and we respond to our boredom, loneliness and internal disorder through distraction and diversion. For many of us, the church represents this life of respectability from which we must occasionally escape by going on "moral holiday." For others of us, the church is itself a distraction and a diversion, a place where we go to play a part, to stroke the ego, to be entertained, to socialize, or to get a little "chicken soup for the soul." Thus, when we are confronted with the addict, we doubt that the gospel has the power that is needed to rescue the addict, for we know that in a very real sense the addict has a fierce and desperate need that is foreign to us and for which we do not have a response.

Like the prophets of old, today's addicts may remind us that our desire for God is trivial and weak, and our horizons of hope and expectancy are limited and mundane. We recoil at the presence of the addict, for we fear that the addict's life is an indictment of the insufficiency of our own lives. The addict has rejected the life of respectable and proximate contentment and demanded instead a life of complete purpose and ecstasy. We recognize that our own lives are not interesting and beautiful enough to offer a genuine alternative to the addict, and we fear that a gospel powerful enough to redeem the addict would also threaten our own lives of decent and decorous mediocrity. We are not sure that we want the church to be a place where persons with addictions are liberated since that would mean that the church is no longer compatible with our own lives. So we characterize addiction as either physical determinism or moral weakness, both of which allow us to ignore the ways in which addiction places our own lives in question.

The question that addiction puts to the church is whether or not it can offer a convincing alternative to the addicted life, and the challenge addiction presents to the church is whether or not it can embody the purposive, ecstatic and all-consuming love of God in a way that is more compelling than the life of addiction. The good news of the gospel is that Jesus came not for those that are healthy but for those that are sick. He came to bring sight to the blind, release to the captive, liberation to the oppressed . . . and new life to the addict. Addiction, because it is so ubiquitous and therefore unavoidable, must force us to ask whether or not we are willing and ready to be a church that embodies Jesus' mission.

To the church that is laid open to the power of the Holy Spirit, addiction is not a threat to be feared but an opportunity to be welcomed. For the good news is that the gospel is powerful to redeem and transform, to break the shackles of every sin, and to liberate us for lives of abundant joy and peace. Because it is so powerfully destructive and death-dealing, addiction provides the church with its most profound invitation to witness to the gospel it proclaims, to make manifest in its own life the resurrection that is its own origin and end. There is therefore no idolatry so potent, no sin so entrenched, no despair so deep, no addiction so inveterate that it is beyond the reach of the Love that has finally and forever triumphed over sin and death: "No, in all these things we are more than conquerors through him who loved us. . . . Neither death, nor life, nor angels, nor rulers, nor things present, nor things to come, nor powers, nor height, nor depth, nor anything else in all creation, will be able to separate us from the love of God in Christ Jesus our Lord" (Rom 8:37-39).

Index

STRATEGIC INITIATIVES IN EVANGELICAL THEOLOGY

Strategic Initiatives in Evangelical Theology is a series of seminal works of scholarship that have strategic relevance for both evangelical scholarship and the evangelical church. They aim to foster interaction within the broader evangelical community and ignite discussion in the wider academic community and around emerging, current, groundbreaking or controversial subjects. The series provides a unique publishing venue for both more senior and younger promising scholars.

While the volumes demonstrate a depth of appreciation for evangelical theology and the current challenges and issues facing it, the series seeks to engage the full range of academic disciplines from theology and biblical studies to history, literature, philosophy, the natural and social sciences, and the arts.

SIET Editorial Advisory Board

Current Titles in the Series

R